STAGES ON THE ROAD

STAGES ON THE ROAD

BY

SIGRID UNDSET

Translated from the Norwegian for the first time by

ARTHUR G. CHATER

Essay Index Reprint Series

 BOOKS FOR LIBRARIES PRESS

FREEPORT, NEW YORK

STANDARD BOOK NUMBER:

8369-1068-0

LIBRARY OF CONGRESS CATALOG CARD NUMBER:

70-80404

PRINTED IN THE UNITED STATES OF AMERICA

PREFACE TO THE ENGLISH EDITION

ALL the articles here collected were originally written for Catholic publications in Norway and Sweden.[1] It goes without saying that very few Catholics here in Scandinavia — whether converts or children of Catholic parents — can have very much knowledge of those pages of the history of the Catholic Church which the officially recognized schoolbooks intentionally or otherwise ignore or distort. Those of our contemporaries who are or who become Catholics are probably occupied, just as much as other people, chiefly by thoughts of their own present and future. They ask whether the Church can offer an explanation of life, a way to salvation from their own most personal distress; they ask whether the Church knows of any way out of the common distress of the whole of humanity. They do not ask about the problems of past ages or the distress of people who died hundreds of years ago, or what was the attitude of the Church towards the problems and the distress of that time, or whether the problems of other ages have any-

[1] The essay on Robert Southwell was first published in *St. Olav*, 1929; that on Margaret Clitherow in the Christmas publication *Kimer, I Klokker* (" Ring out, ye bells ") , 1928; the others in the Scandinavian magazine *Credo* at different dates between 1929 and 1933. — (Tr.) .

v

thing in common with those of our age. Not many people ask whether it is an immutable necessity for human beings — no matter what wealth of experience they may have acquired, no matter how they have increased their material resources and their knowledge of the created world of which they themselves are a part — continually to create circumstances which involve suffering both to themselves and others.

There is an element in the veneration of saints of which Catholics themselves are often unconscious. The cult of saints excludes the cult of success — the veneration of those people who have got on well in this world, the snobbish admiration of wealth and fame. This does not mean that a person who apparently has succeeded in the world and has led a happy life is necessarily a bad Christian who must be prepared for a painful settlement with his God and Judge when he comes to die. But it does mean that the religious business instinct which has caused people to imagine that the material welfare of individuals or nations is a sign of God's special favour, or to see in disasters and defeats a punishment from God — that this is opposed by the Church in her veneration of saints. There is a story of a well-known Norwegian shipowner — I have heard it connected with more than one name, so I dare say it is apocryphal, made up to fit into a fairly common line of thought — anyhow the story goes that the man did not insure his ships; this was supposed to be a proof of his trust in God. Then one day he received news that one of his ships had sunk in spite of this. The man looked up at the ceiling and sighed: " O

Lord God, what have I done wrong — ? " It is human to
think in this way, all too human — and of course a great
number of Catholics yield to the temptation of thinking
so. But it is'a line of thought which the Church herself
disclaims; whenever she celebrates Mass in red vestments it is a protest against this. And even among those
saints who did not become martyrs there are relatively
few who in their lifetime achieved a victory for the
cause for which they had been fighting, if that cause was
of such a nature as to demand realization in external
forms; as, for instance, has been the case with most missionaries and founders of Orders.

Whether Christianity has made it on the whole easier
or more difficult for men to live here on earth is a question on which there will never be agreement. It finally
depends on what we believe about the mystical buoyant
instinct in men from which all religion has originated
— whether it is the answer within us to the call from
a Person — or from personalities — that we can hear
but cannot see, or whether it is a kind of growing
pains in the human race, regarded as an organism
which is impelled from within to grow upwards in
vacant space.

It has been very truly said that not even when the
Church of Christ was at the height of her power in the
eyes of the world was she able to bring about justice and
overcome uncharitableness among men. Even in those
times when most men firmly believed in Heaven and Hell
there were always plenty of them who preferred to brave
the threat of Hell rather than renounce the joys of self-

worship, the gratification of hatred and power, or sub-
ordinate themselves to a force to which their whole ego
was antagonistic. The position is this, that the Christian
Church can never have the right to suppress what her
Founder has said about eternal perdition. But it is
equally certain that what the Church has achieved has
not been achieved by frightened instruments who shrank
in slavish terror before the wrath of a cruel God. She
has accomplished it through her saints who had the
heroic love of God — of the Uncreated Creator and of
the created world, in which the fight is for or against
God. The sectarian animosity against the cult of saints
is one of the reasons which have made it possible to
represent Christianity as a religion of fear, not of
heroism.

A great deal of the matter in the present book will not
be new to English-speaking readers — at all events not
to English Catholics. To Norwegian readers it was for
the most part entirely unknown. And the essays were
written partly with the object of making Norwegian
readers acquainted with pages of history with which,
for good reasons, the public in a Protestant country has
been kept in ignorance. To give any complete list of the
various authorities I have used in the preparation of
these studies is no longer possible. A great many of them
are English — for the articles on Margaret Clitherow
and Robert Southwell I have used all the monographs
I could come across, besides more comprehensive works
on the history of England during the century of the
Reformation. My interest in Angela Merici and her

struggle in the cause of women is due to my reading her life by Sister Mary Monica, of St. Martin, Ohio. This led to my getting all the available books about the history of the Order in Europe.

Sigrid Undset.

Lillehammer, May 1934.

CONTENTS

RAMÓN LULL OF PALMA

 " INFIDEL DOG! " thundered the knight, flashing a lightning glance at his captive. — And then as a rule the knight proceeds in the same strain with his thunders and lightnings. If the captive is unlucky enough to be a Jew, he will subsequently be taken in hand by the knight's dentist, and dental treatment in the Middle Ages was even more unpleasant than it is now. The captive is just as likely to be a Mohammedan, a Saracen, and then as often as not he enjoys the author's sympathy and is given an opportunity of showing his superiority to the poor rude and superstitious Crusader both in culture and nobility. Indeed, the relations between Christians, Mohammedans and Jews appeared no more complicated than this to many authors of the nineteenth century.

People of the nineteenth century showed in fact a quite extraordinary degree of incapacity when they tried to understand the men and women of the Middle Ages, even when they went about it with the best of wills. I had almost said that in this case they failed most miserably; no misunderstanding has so disturbing an effect as mistaken enthusiasm. And in the nineteenth century people were really enthusiastic about certain manifestations of the spirit of the Middle Ages, so far as they were capable of discerning and misunderstanding it — mediæval architecture for instance. People had discovered that Gothic was something more than a disorderly ugliness, a regrettable barbaric intermezzo between the representationist formality of late antiquity and the renaissance attempts to put the clock back — to cut a thousand years of development out of the history of Europe and aim at a linking-up with the ideas of a distant past, to prune Christianity right down to its roots and start again where primitive Christianity leaves off, a thing which the Reformers imagined to be possible. The Romanticists had a great fancy for mediæval ruins: all over Europe they built sham ruins and restored those that remained — often according to the principle followed in tricking out a fine Swedish manor-house of the early eighteenth century in Victorian Gothic. The effect of this was described by a friend of mine by alleging that he had seen this inscription set up over the brand-new feudal gateway: " Anno 1875 Wart denna Gambla Gåhrden giorth mycket Gamblare." [1] New Gothic churches and town-halls and castellated villas were thickly sown over Germany and England. And here in the North we followed the fashion as well as we could: the open-air museum on Bygdö has a lovely collection

[1] " Anno 1875 Was thys Olde Hous y-maked moche Oldere." — (Tr.)

4

of our great-grandfathers' Gothic chairs with traceried backs and bead-embroidered seats. And close by is the resplendent Oscarshall, white and dainty as though made of sugar.

The fashion for Gothic was of course like all fashions a symptom of a contemporary spiritual attitude. At the beginning of the century it looked as if revolution and war had made a clean sweep of the world of the immediately preceding generations — the palaces and prisons of absolutism and the academies and ornamental gardens of the age of enlightenment. The young felt themselves to be a chosen generation, called to rebuild the world, more beautiful and better than before. Young minds of the *Sturm und Drang* period yearned for an outlook on life which should embrace the whole creation as a unity and at the same time open a way to infinity. " Through the ego leads the vast stairway, from the lichens on the rocks to the seraphs " — but the ego is not the individual ego of each little human being, it has become conscious of being a radiation from the eternal will which draws everything upward and binds everything together. It then dawned upon some of them that the outlook they were striving to formulate had points of contact with the mediæval view of the world. And because they felt the need of expressing their new outlook more rapidly and more strikingly than could be done by statement and explanation, they resorted to images and symbols and parables — and discovered that much of what had been scoffed at by the rationalists as mediæval childishness, crudity, and the outcome of a

5

silly superstition, was in fact nothing but the symbols and emblems of that age. It had simply appeared meaningless to the people of the age of enlightenment in the same way as stenography looks like a meaningless scribble to those who know nothing of shorthand systems.

Nevertheless the nineteenth century only arrived at a very imperfect interpretation of the mediæval shorthand signs. The reaction which set in after the Napoleonic wars, the reappearance in new forms of the ideas of the French revolution, the iron age of capitalism, the changed character of science and the practical results it led to — all this tended to thrust an interest in the Middle Ages into the background. The historians continued to unearth, collect and revise ever-increasing masses of material, researchers were at work on popular tradition, architects went on restoring and imitating mediæval buildings, poets chose subjects from the Middle Ages for historical dramas and unhistorical romances and ballads. But their understanding failed them on a vital point — that of the religion of the Middle Ages, in other words their very outlook on life.

To a certain extent this applies also to the Catholics. For centuries the Church had been forced back into a defensive position, even in countries where it was the only officially recognized Church. In the face of a growing absolutism in the State it had often been *compelled* to show pliancy: the Church's first duty must always be the care of the souls of those human beings who are alive here and now; they have the right to demand that it shall administer the sacraments to them and teach

6

them the way, the truth and the life. It can only work for the generations yet unborn through those who are to be their progenitors, so far as this can be done without detriment to the souls of the living. And the Church had superabundant experience of how effectively the autocratic kings and princes of the new age could deprive their Catholic subjects of the sacrifice of the mass and the true doctrine, when for one reason or another they themselves had broken loose from Catholic Christendom. It had seen how the protestant national churches tended more and more to serve primarily a worldly aim — that of making people into good and obedient citizens under the autocracy, first of kings, and later of constitutions. It was not only in Norway that the royal cipher of the Oldenborgs was given rank and position in the churches equal with the cross and the Lamb of God, the chalice and the symbols of the apostles. In rendering to Cæsar what was Cæsar's they had thus given God almost all that He had a claim to. That all authority is of God no longer meant that the rulers merely exercise authority *by virtue of God's grace and mercy* — it tended more and more to imply that God and the Authorities were in a mystical way allied against the subjects, whose first duty was obedience. Time after time the Church was forced to be silent and tolerant — but time after time, on the other hand, its servants were pliant to the point of complicity and indulgent to the point of shamelessness in dealing with the sins of those in power. It is not so strange therefore that the mass of Catholics, who shared the faith and the fundamental out-

7

look on existence of the Middle Ages, but who saw the world as from an entrenchment or through the loopholes of a fortress — with an extremely limited field of view — should have fantastic dreams about the position of the Church in the social life of the Middle Ages, about the time when hardly anyone doubted the objective truth of the Church's explanation of human life and destiny. At that time the Church stood in the centre of living life. But the ideas that were entertained of its powerful position in the Middle Ages were false and exaggerated. It had been involved in ceaseless conflict: scarcely had the semi-barbarian hordes of the Great Migrations begun to settle down and take root in their new homes, so that the work of their evangelization could be carried on more or less according to plan, than fresh invaders broke in upon Europe from the East, Huns, Avars, Tatars, driving the fugitive peoples before them into fresh migrations. Islam conquered the Christian centres of culture at the eastern end of the Mediterranean, in North Africa and in the Pyrenean peninsula, and gained a foothold time after time in the countries north of the Mediterranean. In reality, for the greater part of the Middle Ages Christendom was like an island between a sea of hostile peoples and the ocean to the west and north. And within Christendom itself there was ceaseless revolt against the authority which the Church claimed over the faithful — the heretics denied the authority of its teaching, emperors and kings and princes denied its right to interfere in the development of social conditions. And rich and poor, high and low, laymen and the Church's own consecrated servants rebelled alike against its doctrine of morals; they defied it openly and sabotaged it in secret, and wherever anyone started a defection from Christian morality he was followed by the cheerful crowd who think they can surely do wrong if others can. People of the last century naturally found it particularly difficult to understand this — that so many who believed the Church to be the mouthpiece of God's revealed truth should act in direct opposition to what this doctrine declared to be necessary for the salvation of their souls. The very concepts of truth and truth-seeking, in matters of faith and morality, had undergone such a change that most people assumed religious and moral truths to be things to which each individual felt his own way — in contradistinction to the truths of natural science which can be proved (and which at that time very few people imagined might be insufficiently proved owing to fallacious deductions or inadequate data). Thus one feels one's way to the sect or the personal conviction or the attitude to religion which is least liable to expose the individual to demands against which his whole nature tempts him to revolt. The hypocrite, the man who pretends to believe and love and honour what in reality he has rejected or regards with indifference, who lives and acts according to principles quite different from those he acknowledges with his lips, is not of course a type peculiar to recent times. The history of the Middle Ages swarms with political hypocrites, traitorous princes and traitorous vassals, disloyal friends and kinsmen —

9

princes of the Church and temporal lords feign friend-
ship, while meditating treachery against one another;
in their convents monks and nuns feign obedience and
brotherly love, while intriguing for election to positions
and favours within their house or Order. But it would
be an error to believe that even the most depraved
prelates or priests of the Middle Ages were always hypo-
critical in preaching a faith which they did not follow
in their lives. By far the greater part of them certainly
believed in what they taught — and knew what they
were doing when they followed their own nature, which
refused to submit to the commandments of their doctrine. There is a good deal that is misleading in what
we have been told about the people of the Middle Ages
being lashed into obedience by the fear of hell; many
of them argued with Aucassin: " To Paradise go none
but the old priests and the palsied dotards and cripples
who crouch day and night before the altars and in the
ancient crypts . . . folk who are naked and barefoot
and full of sores, folk who are dying of cold and hunger
and misery. . . . To hell go the handsome clerics and
the goodly knights who meet their death in tourneys
and in the sport of war . . . and thither go the fair and
courteous ladies who besides their husbands have two
or three friends, and thither go the gold and silver and
rich furs and minever and the harpers and minstrels and
all the kings of this world. With them will I go —."
Dante's hell is the place where individualism celebrates
its supreme triumphs — the damned have renounced
all but the ego which it is their sole desire to cultivate;

they suffer punishment for their rebellion against the universal harmony of Eternal Love, but that for which they exposed themselves to damnation does not injure all-loving Omnipotence: Farinata degli Uberti retains his pride in the midst of his torments; the adulteress Francesca da Rimini soars over the gulf of hell clasped in an eternal embrace with the man for whom she gave her salvation; Brunetto Latini, who kindled the passion for beauty and knowledge and poetry in so many young minds, and corrupted certain of his favourite disciples with secret vices, runs over the glowing sands like "a victor in the races at Verona." The scoffer continues to scoff; Ciampolo, who when alive grew rich by corrupt traffic in official posts, cheats the demons who carry out the sentence upon him; "What once I was alive, that am I dead," says Capaneus, the blasphemer. Since God gave men a free will, there *must* be a hell — for him who loves himself more than God it would be worse to have to *worship* Him in heaven. *That* was the mediæval idea of the egocentric cult of personality — God's Only-begotten Son came into the world to *win* souls, not to take them by force.

In the Middle Ages, as now and always, the place of the Church triumphant was in Heaven (and she does not force her enemies to take part in her triumph!). The Church upon earth is a Church militant. But the Church militant of the Middle Ages had a full and living sense of the Church's unity: the Church suffering in Purgatory, the Church militant on earth, and the Church triumphant in Heaven are *one*. People did not merely believe this; it was a thing they felt in the very marrow of their souls. And many of those people of the Middle Ages who were believing Catholics and committed all the grave sins against which the Church admonished them, must have hoped they would nevertheless be saved in the end, through the intercessions of the poor which they had bought by alms, and through those of the Church for which they had also paid cash — like the man in the Gospel who was paralysed, but whose friends brought him to Jesus on a mattress, and when they could not enter by the door of the house where the Saviour was, they climbed up to the roof, made a hole in it and let the sick man down. — *This* is, and has always been, the moral danger with Catholicism: that we all more or less consciously harbour a thought at the back of our minds that we shall not be allowed to stray quite so far from God's purpose with us as we are struggling to do with the conscious part of our ego. Someone who has been capable of a much closer assimilation to Christ than we ourselves cared or had courage to achieve, will drag us into the presence of His mercy and lay us before His feet — some poor people whom we helped and whose gratitude was more unselfish than our generosity, a little child who died in a state of innocence, the saints whom we invoked in moments when we had a clearer vision than usual of our real selves. — It is of course a moral danger to rely on the aid of others' intercessions. But what has put the idea into people's heads that in this dangerous life of ours the most important thing of all, our religion, should be free from danger?

But in those days people did not merely pray for their dead and pray to the saints just as naturally as they went to their neighbours to borrow a light when their fire had gone out at home. They also talked about the saints as folk in all ages have talked about their neighbours. That is to say, a mass of misapprehensions and rumours were in circulation about them, which in some cases had a basis of fact and in others were pure fiction. People related legends about saints of both sexes with just as much calm assurance as the people of our day make up legends about film stars, for instance. But since the time of the Reformers the Church had been unceasingly charged in non-Catholic quarters with dealing in lies — its dogmas were the work of men, its pretensions false, its priests and monks had stuffed the people with fables in order to keep them under and fleece them, in all times and places. In reply to such challenges as these many of the defenders of Catholicism were not content with confuting Protestant attacks on the Catholic truths. They were ready to defend every possible or impossible individual opinion, bearing the stamp of its time, which had been put forward in the course of the ages by Catholic personages of note, as though these had been definite dogmas. And they were unwilling to admit that any romance of a saint, however fantastic, might be a romance and not a sober report of facts. For that matter their reaction was no different from that of everyone else,

I 3

whenever, for instance, doubts are cast on the authenticity of a nation's legendary history.

We may be sure that the people of the Middle Ages themselves did not always take their legends so literally. It is clear that a collection of legendary material such as that which is called in Old Norse *Mariu Saga* contains legends of at least two different types. The brief and artless narratives of some such occurrence as the extinction of a fire or the freeing of a district from a plague of wolves or the remarkable cure of a sick person after prayers had been offered for the intercession of the Virgin Mary, are evidently reports of an event as it took place, or as people believed it to have taken place. The novel-like legends of a conflict among several people, a tragic love affair, or a moral conflict in the soul of an individual, are stories of another kind. They are often told with great charm, and their denouement enforces some ethical or religious point or other. It is inconceivable that the people who wrote down these legends should not themselves have perceived that they were dealing with two different kinds of story. Of course this need not have prevented many of their readers and listeners from " believing " in the truth of both types of legend, just as for instance masses of the readers of missionary magazines and Christian weeklies " believe " not only in reports and statistics but also in the edifying serials about pious negroes and converted drunkards, without reflecting that they have before them different kinds of improving matter. It is obvious that the legends were in great part tendentious *fiction*. But even more

I 4

than that, they were the manifestation of an eternally human tendency — the love of romancing, the desire of knowing a good deal about the private affairs of celebrated personages, and the longing of individuals to be able to say that they had had personal contact with such and such a celebrity and had proof that the great person took a special interest in one's own ego! This last factor may well have given rise to not a few stories of miracles. Local patriotism too played a certain part — " you know, the old bishop who lies buried in *our* parish church, he was one of the holiest of the holy; Our Lord won't say no to anything he prays for."

In so far as this wild growth of legend-making was subjected to any criticism at all, it was the clergy who were its critics. It is characteristic that Norwegian historians, for example, have calmly assumed from one generation to another that it was " the clergy " who from motives of publicity declared that the eclipse of the sun of August 31, 1030, occurred during the battle of Stiklestad. As J. D. Landmark has shown, ecclesiastical tradition evidently knew nothing whatever of an eclipse having taken place during the battle; he has proved that the legend did not originate in Norway at all, but in Iceland, and was not known in this country until a century and a half after St. Olav's death, through the works of Icelandic poets and saga-writers. In England we have the story of the monks of Glastonbury who entirely dissociated themselves from the legend that Joseph of Arimathæa was buried in their precincts, which did not deter King Edward III from causing official search to be made for the grave. In Ireland the story of St. Patrick's Purgatory is well known; it was by order of the Pope that the famous cave on an island in Lough Derg was filled in, after a Dutch pilgrim believed he had discovered that the people who alleged they had witnessed strange things in the cave had only been dreaming, and that the whole affair was a fraud. Indeed, all through the Middle Ages the Papacy endeavoured, directly and through the bishops, to exercise some control over those whom popular opinion declared to be holy, even if it was not till 1634 that Urban VIII decreed that no public worship was to be accorded to new saints until their case had been investigated by the Apostolic See.

But if the Catholics of last century imagined the faith of " the age of faith " as something far more tame and submissive than it was, and made an honest effort to accept literally a mass of legends which originally had certainly never been regarded as literally true, the non-Catholics were entirely bewildered by the same material. And it became proportionally more difficult for them to understand anything of the essence of saint-worship, as the sum of Christian ideas inherited by Protestantism gradually fell to pieces — being replaced by separatist opinions and subjective convictions and religious sentiment. For the Reformers were convinced that they had grasped what the revealed God had intended to reveal so clearly and plainly that no one who did not agree with them had any notion of what true Christianity was. They then endowed their image of God with the same arrogance that caused them to decline the intercession of the saints — to them it was inconceivable that God might be willing to act through men who had become like Christ, might without jealousy transmit a part of His omnipotence to faithful servants. Nothing could be farther from them than the kind of self-knowledge which caused so many saints to doubt the divine origin of all the visions they saw and all the voices they heard and the apparent miracles which they performed while alive — most saints were fully aware that the devil was able to imitate all such phenomena. The gay humility which prompted St. Francis and the first friars minor to say, as though with a shrug of the shoulders: " Well, if we work miracles it must be because God wishes to show that He can use not merely the most excellent, but just as easily the frailest instruments to do His work " — that was very remote from the Reformers' mentality. And in proportion as the very concept of God grew more and more blurred in the Protestant world, and it was even looked upon as a sign of true spirituality to assert the impossibility of the human mind forming conceptions of God, it was entirely forgotten that the Middle Ages had preached without ceasing *how* incomprehensible God is: He Himself has taken the initiative and communicated to us every atom of what we know about Him, by both natural and supernatural means. The division between the uncreated Creator and all created things, from primal matter to the holy Virgin, can only be overstepped by her and by all men because God intervenes and draws His creature back to Himself; if men may themselves work at their

1 7

own sanctification and help others to sanctify themselves, it is because God has willed that it should be so.
God has willed once for all that the rain should fall
from clouds — He could undoubtedly have arranged
the question of irrigation in another way. God could
have saved mankind without taking a little Jewish girl
from Nazareth into collaboration — but as it was He
sent His angel to her and gave to her answer: " Behold
the handmaid of the Lord," the significance it acquired.
The hypothesis that the saints are divinities in disguise
rests on a misunderstanding: people knew very well that
all holy men are human, not divine-born. On the contrary, the old gods sometimes had to put up with being
reduced to mortals and even to being hailed as model
Christians — when people continued to regard their
ancient holy places with affection but asserted that no
faun had ever haunted this spot, far from it: a pious
Christian soldier was murdered here for refusing to
deny Christ, or when they deposed the ancient water-
spirit of a holy well and declared that the water owed
its virtue to the prayers of a pious virgin.

As State Christianity became reduced more and more
to a kind of justification of the life and opinions of " decent people," there was added a positive hatred of the
sort of holiness which the saints had practised — since
it had notoriously caused them to reject a number of
good things which were greatly prized by the community, to comport themselves in an eccentric fashion and
to snap their fingers at custom and convention. Moreover many of the holy men and women had such a past

as we are bound to believe God may forgive, but decent people never.

People in the Protestant countries had now been disciplined for centuries into the view of the Reformation which here in Norway has been expressed so forcibly by the poet from Hadeland:

When Rome her Despot took away
And Denmark sent thee in his place
An earthly God, a crownèd Friend,
Began for thee the crownèd days.

It is true that since Sören Möller's time our views of Christian III's benefactions to Norway and of the worldly-divine dynasty of the Oldenborgs as a whole have changed not a little. There has even appeared a sporadic inclination to recognize the men of the Catholic hierarchy under the first kings of united Denmark-Norway as in some sort pioneers of Norwegian nationalism. This is an error. No doubt the policy of these Norwegian churchmen was marked throughout by distrust of the Danes, but otherwise it is vague enough, or at any rate we find it difficult to trace any clear lines in it. But naturally the task of the clergy was in the first place to preserve the true faith among the people, and to defend the liberty of the Church against the encroachments of the worldly authorities — and the clergy's weakness was the eternally human disposition to confuse private aims with a life's mission. It is true that the clergy was more national in the sense that in

Norway both secular priests and conventuals were drawn from the most various classes of society, whereas after the Reformation there arose before very long what were called clerical families, in which sons and sons-in-law commonly acquired a sort of prescriptive right to succeed their fathers in office. And as the ministry was now nothing but a department of officialdom, it received in common with other departments a very scanty supply of fresh blood from other sections of the community. Now this is undeniably a state of things which occurs fairly constantly wherever a priesthood is not hindered by a rule of celibacy from forming dynasties — and even within the Roman Catholic Church the obstacle was evaded in many ways: by nepotism, by dispensations from the rule that priests must be of legitimate birth, so as to admit illegitimate sons of priests to the service of the Church, by families who had founded prebends or given estates to monasteries contriving to assert a kind of prior claim whereby their members could enjoy these prebends or be cared for in these monasteries. One of the causes of the decay of monastic life in the late Middle Ages was in fact the endowment of religious houses with all these revenues, which in reality might almost be regarded as family bequests. Nothing therefore can be more unhistorical than the assertion that the *people* in different countries wished to see the celibacy of the clergy abolished — it was the discontented and misplaced priests and monks and nuns who wished it. The people were indignant that the rule was *not* enforced; what they demanded was a clergy that kept its vows, priests who were really willing to be everything to everyone, monks and nuns who were really poor and chaste and kept watch in their prayers for all weak and sick and sinful Christian souls. And where the people actually saw the old ideals realized there was no change in their feelings towards them — in countries like England, for instance, where monastic life was still to a great extent healthy, it was precisely the mass of the people in the country-side who were most ready to hazard their lives in the struggle against the tyranny of the despoilers of the Church.

What above all necessitated the energetic anti-Catholic propaganda was that the "Reformation" which ensued was no reformation of the Church but a new formation, which was in keeping with the taste and feelings of the rising middle class. It *needed* a vast and unscrupulous propaganda before it could make any pretence of being an "improvement" of the Church in other circles than just that section of the nobility which received its share of Church and monastic estates, and on the other hand the middle-class townsmen. The revolts of communistic character which at the time of the Reformation broke out here and there in country districts, where the peasants' distress had become intolerable, were directed in the main against the owners of estates, including the great clerical landowners — but the Reformers, with Luther himself at their head, cried out more loudly than anyone else for their suppression with fire and sword. Catholicism has compromised — far too much — with the narrow shopkeeper outlook

which was the final product of the spirit of the Renaissance and the Reformation. But Protestantism was a
product of this very mentality — which also explains
how it came to imagine itself akin to the spirit of the
primitive Church, to the first little congregations in the
cities of the Roman Empire, and to reject as a perversion the whole development through which Christendom had passed since it had come to include the people
of the country districts and the warriors, farmers and
seamen of the Great Migrations. When a feeling for
nature reappears within the Protestant world it does so
as a subjective and æstheticizing sentiment — the hymn-
writers are religiously affected by impressions of a childhood spent in country parsonages. It is nevertheless as
remote as can be from the Catholic recognition of the
community of man with nature, which caused the
Church to adopt the immemorial pagan festivals of
solstice and seed-time and harvest in her calendar and
make them into processional days, when priest and congregation pass round the fields and pray the Almighty
not merely for a good year and peace, but also for preservation from the snares of the devil and for a blessed
death — or pronounce a benediction upon cattle and
farm implements, consecrate meadows and healing
herbs, set up crucifixes at crossways and place the peasant's working year in the hands of a whole celestial department of agriculture composed of tutelary saints.

Sometimes in the same breath, at other times from
different quarters, the Catholic Church has been accused of having extirpated pagan elements of culture

with the direst fanaticism and of having assimilated pagan elements of culture! There is some truth in the accusation — if we choose to call it an accusation. The champions of Catholic Christianity tore down heathen temples, fulminated against the prostitution of the fertility cults and tried as energetically as they could to efface the very traces of human sacrifice. And they assimilated the spring and harvest festivals of the fertility cult, redirected the ancient worship of sources and holy mountains and groves. For in fact, as Catholic missionaries have insisted, people who have no knowledge of the Creator of the Universe do better to worship springs and trees and rocks — even if their worship be accompanied by grotesque rites and addressed to an idol — than to go about among the wonders of the world without fear or reverence, devotion or amazement. Chapels were built not merely in places which had already been sacred in pagan times. In regions of ancient Catholic culture we find pilgrimage churches and Calvarys and oratories whose purpose is to remind the wayfarer to pray, or at least to remember his Saviour for a moment — they lie dotted along the roads and paths, within the woods and on bare crags among the mountains, from which one has a wide view and where they can be seen from a great distance.

We must remember that humility, which St. Catherine calls the marrow of the faithful soul, is not based on consciousness of sin — as non-Christians, and often Protestants too, try to make out. *We* can arrive at the virtue of humility *through* acknowledgment of sin, which teaches us to see ourselves in a sober light. But the Blessed Virgin is held up to us as the pattern of humility — and it is our faith that she is undefiled by sin. And Jesus says of Himself: " I am meek and humble of heart." *His* humility is the stupendous mystery in which our thought is drowned in the inconceivable light of the Uncreate. The Creator bends to the state of the created as to a yoke. (To those who do not believe in the divinity of Christ these words of Jesus must be just as meaningless as so many others — just as over-weening as would be His promise of forgiveness of sins against God and against fellow-men, were He not Him-self the One sinned against in all sins.)

Humility is the acknowledgment of the relation between Him who creates and that which the Creator has created. Growth in humility means an intensification of this acknowledgment; God works, we are His work — our works are a manipulation of material which has been given us, every scrap of it, with tools which we have received as a gift. Original sin is the attempt to deny this abysmal difference between the Power which acts and its work — " You shall be as God," says the Tempter. It is from the holy humility of his soul that St. Francis speaks of our brother the sun — my lord brother Sun, he says, as one king speaking of another. " Benedicite, omnia opera Domini, Domino," — thus begins the hymn of praise of Ananias, Azarias and Misael, that part of it which the Church has included in the liturgy of morning prayer; and then it calls upon all created things to praise the Lord, angels and heavens,

2 4

sun and moon, cold and heat, ice and snow and light-
nings and clouds, mountains and hills and all things
that spring up in the earth, fountains and seas and the
whales that move in the waters and the fowls of the air,
wild beasts and cattle and the spirits and souls of the
just. To be allowed to see God, the source from which
all things have proceeded — that is the bliss which is
promised to the pure in heart. The supernatural life
which was given to man when God created him in His
image, which man forfeited when he wished to be as
God, the image as the Master who made it — could only
be given back by God Himself. "Now this is eternal
life: that they may know Thee, the only true God, and
Jesus Christ, whom Thou hast sent."

"*Paiens ont tort et Chrétiens ont droit*," so ring the
words of the Chanson de Roland — and this is the fundamental conviction on which people lived in the Middle Ages. Christians are right, because what they believe
in is not a construction of their own thoughts and impulses and emotions — on all such things the beliefs of
the pagans were founded — but the Christian believes
in something which has been revealed by the only One
who knows all about all things, God. Not that there
were no sceptics even in the Middle Ages who doubted
the whole story of a divine revelation or who found
difficulty in believing this or that article of what was
revealed. This did not necessarily mean that the doubter
was a heretic — it is not doubt which makes a man a
heretic, but belief; belief, that is, in his own subjective
religious experiences, or in his having received separate

2 5

enlightenment from Our Lord. Of course it will not do
to carry generalization too far in speaking of the people
of the Middle Ages; the same differences existed among
them as we find at the present day — differences between clever and stupid, sensitive and coarse people,
between cultivated and uncultivated intelligences. But
there is a little story in Joinville's chronicle of St. Louis
which throws light on the ideas of an intelligent and
sensitive mediæval person on the subject of doubt:

An eminent cleric confesses to Bishop Guillaume of
Paris (1228–48) that he is unable to believe the doctrine of the Church concerning the holy Sacrament of
the Altar. The bishop asks him whether he finds pleasure in being tempted by the Devil in this way. To
which the other replies hotly: No, it tortures him un-
speakably. Then the bishop says: " You know that the
King of France is at war with the King of England. And
the castle which lies nearest the border in Poitou is la
Rochelle. Now I ask you — if the King had charged you
with holding for him la Rochelle, which lies on the
exposed frontier, and me with holding the castle of
Montlhéri in the heart of France, in a peaceful district
— to which of us would the King be the more grateful
when the war was over, to you who had held la Rochelle
for him and not lost it, or to me who had held Montlhéri for him and not lost it? — My heart," says Bishop
Guillaume, " may be likened to the castle of Montlhéri;
I have not been affected by doubts of the Sacrament of
the Altar. Therefore I say to you, if God is grateful to
me for believing firmly and steadfastly, He will show

2 6

you fourfold gratitude for preserving your heart for Him in the war of temptation. — You may be of good cheer, for your conduct is more pleasing to Our Lord than mine."

In our day no doubt we have all heard something about religious psychology. Antireligious psychology has been less thoroughly investigated. The Middle Ages knew more about that. If the human *will* played no part in a soul's acceptance or rejection of grace, there would be no sense in the saying of Christ: " He that believeth and is baptized shall be saved: but he that believeth not shall be condemned."

Nor was the Christian view of Islam and Judaism so simple and undiscriminating as it has often been represented in history books of the good old days of enlightenment and liberalism. For that matter, the circumstances were not of so simple a nature as to be explicable on a basis of religious antagonism and religious fanaticism alone. It was not merely the Holy Land and the Holy Sepulchre that had fallen into the hands of the infidels. The centres of civilization of the early Church had been submerged by the conquerors from the East — and the mediæval theologians were familiar with their Fathers, the voices from Tagaste and Carthage, Alexandria and Antioch. Memories were still alive of the time when the Mediterranean had been an inland sea in the midst of Christendom, on which Christians could pass to and fro in comparative security — the object of the Crusades was *re*-conquest, both spiritual and material.

Nor does it exhaust the question to say that the mediæval persecutions of Jews are merely to be referred
to primitive men's hatred of " the murderers of Christ,"
or to the greed of rapacious princes for the fortunes
amassed by Jews wherever they found a temporary asy-
lum. Even before the destruction of Palestine as a Jewish country the greater part of the Jewish people had
been living abroad, mainly in the cities of the Roman
Empire. The young European peoples of the Middle
Ages were agricultural communities with an upper
class of landed nobility. The peasant's distrust of townsmen, the countryman's suspicion that financiers are all
more or less rogues and extortioners, were no doubt
contributory factors. And the Church was there with her
canonical interdict of usury, about which the Jews had
no need to trouble themselves. Where kings and princes
opened the doors of their countries to the Jews and
made use of them as financiers, as physicians and as dip-
lomats, there always arose among the people a feeling
that the Jews are — not *more* gifted than Europeans,
for there is always present a conviction that Europeans
are superior to Jews in spheres which it is difficult to
characterize. But it is none the less true that the Jews
possess powers of concentration, are clearer-sighted at
short range, have greater adaptability. And when out-
bursts of hatred occur in places where Jews have been
allowed to establish themselves, this hatred is usually a
mixture of dislike of the alien element which we have
never quite been able to understand and of suppressed
self-hatred — since persecutions of Jews nearly always

2 8

imply a breach of promises and agreements. So religious fanaticism is called upon to deaden the shame of having allowed oneself to be tricked, as well as that of having broken one's promises. And behind this alien people in Europe — a migratory people with an excellent system of mutual communication and information — stood the idea of powerful Jewish rulers in the camp of the enemy, Islam. And beyond the boundaries of Christendom there were rumours of mighty independent Jewish realms: to the south of Ethiopia the tribes of Dan, Naphtali and Asser were said to form a nation of warriors and priests; on the borders of Persia nomads of the race of Ruben, Ephraim and Manasses controlled vast territories. Many modern investigators are disposed to believe in a historical foundation for these reports. The Khozars of the Crimea are well known; they were Tatars who had been converted to Judaism and were ruled by a Jewish king.

There was yet another essential reason for the animosity between Jews and Christians. The books of the Old Testament are at the same time the holy Scriptures of the Catholic Church. From the prophecies and chronicles of the Old Testament the Lessons are taken, which form part of the liturgy and are included in priests' breviaries. The Psalms of David are also the prayer-book of the Catholic Church. The Canticle and the Book of Wisdom were in favour as religious reading and were interpreted and paraphrased and rendered into verse and prose in the language of the people. To Catholic Christians it seemed so obvious that all these writings were prophetic of the incarnation of Christ, treated of a historical development leading up to Him. Christianity is the true Israel, the heir, the true-born son of " the free woman " — and Israelites by birth and blood who possess the same scriptures and know them by heart, but yet will not understand their obvious meaning, must be perverse and hardened. But in the eyes of the Jews Jesus of Nazareth necessarily appeared a traitor to the traditions of God's chosen people — His followers were apostates and strangers, and now they were persecuting God's peculiar people.

Racial animosity no doubt played its part; the European peoples were compounded of essentially different elements from the Anatolian-Semitic, Jews and Arabs. But no theory entered into the question. There are abundant examples of Europeans in their intercourse with Mohammedans having been quite aware of the valuable personal qualities of their opponents and full of admiration for the Orientals' superiority in learning and material civilization. Contempt for the boorish Western knights and lords is more manifest on the part of the Orientals (and the Byzantines). When we think of how persistently the Catholic Church has been accused of having beaten into its adherents an unhealthy shame of the human body and all natural functions, it is amusing to come across in Arab writers the most inordinate contempt for the Christians' immodesty in all that concerns sexual life, their failure to understand the degradation of exposing oneself. It is not merely the profligacy of the Christians which appears bestially coarse to men brought up in the harem tradition — the lack of privacy in their family life, the way in which they allow their women to appear in public and to interfere in the affairs of men, even their bathing customs, seem abominable and shameless in the eyes of the Arabs.

Turning to the Jews, we find that Jewish converts to Christianity were received with enthusiasm, often amounting to fond indulgence — except where it was a case of mass-conversion, when there was reason to conclude, or when it appeared later, that the change of religion was only a pretence. If there was ground for believing that a Jew had really acknowledged Christ as his Saviour and Mary as the mother of God, he was usually greeted with heartfelt joy and accepted without reserve as a fellow-Christian. Many Jewish converts were destined to play a conspicuous part in their new surroundings — even among the clergy. Cardinal Pier Pierleone, who was elected Pope by the priesthood of Rome — his election was uncanonical and invalid, and he is reckoned among the Antipopes under the name of Anacletus II — was the son of a Jewish convert. Nor was any superstition current in those days that Jews were wanting in physical courage or military talent, when as fellow-citizens they were given an opportunity of showing these qualities. Samuel Chrzanowski, who in 1675 defended the fortress of Trembowla against the Turks, and his equally heroic wife Sofia, were baptized Jews, and they had their counterparts also in the Middle Ages.

Human consciousness still regarded difference of religion as the most profound antagonism among the nations, and other causes of hostility were of less account. It was the belief of the majority that, if the Catholic Church could gather all peoples into her embrace, there would be, if not peace on earth, at any rate more peace and unity, less misery in the world, and the hosts of the blessed in Heaven would be infinitely multiplied.

2

FOR over four hundred years the Balearic Isles had been in the hands of the Moors. Time after time expeditions from Christian countries had attempted to recover these nests of pirates, which made the sea and its coasts insecure over a wide region. Sigurd the Crusader [1] had tried his strength here, in skirmishes on Formentera and Minorca.

On New Year's Eve 1229 King Jacme the Conqueror of Aragon captured the chief town of Majorca. (It was given the name of Palma later.) He built the cathedral there, founded monasteries and gave land to the Knights Hospitallers, to the Templars and to many of the knights who had taken part in his campaign against the islands. One of them bore the name of Ramón Lull, a Catalan belonging to an old noble family which owned estates in the neighbourhood of Barcelona. He settled in Majorca for good, and his famous son, Ramón Lull the younger, was born at Palma. The date of his birth is variously

[1] Sigurd Jorsalfar (" Jerusalem-farer "), King of Norway, 1103–1130. — (Tr.)

given, between 1232 and 1235. He was doubtless the only son.

He was educated at court with the two sons of King Jacme — owing, so tradition says, to Queen Violante being charmed with the boy's good looks and talents. He cannot have been fully grown when he was made a kind of tutor to the younger of the princes, Don Jacme; the pupil was only ten years his junior. When Prince Jacme was acclaimed as the future lord of Majorca, Ramón became his seneschal and chamberlain. He was then about twenty-two or twenty-three. Handsome and spoilt, an adept in all knightly sports, a good dancer and singer and troubadour, he led a wild life at this time — he says himself he was a scoffer and a blasphemer, often false to his friends, and an insatiable woman-hunter. " The beauty of women, O Lord, has been as a sickness and a calamity upon my eyes, for it was the beauty of women that caused me to forget Thy great goodness and the beauty of Thy works."

The King found him a wealthy and handsome bride, Blanca Picany; he hoped that Ramón might be a little less profligate when married. The hope was not realized. But he had two children by his wife, Dominic and Magdalena. He spent much time in travelling with the court during these years, in France and in the King's Spanish dominions. Ramón's love of adventure and thirst for beauty were abundantly fostered at this youthful period.

Legends have grown luxuriantly about the figure of Ramón, though the actual facts of his life are better known than is the case with many of his contemporaries

3 3

— his writings abound in autobiographical touches. I reproduce here the romantic legend of his conversion, since it has been treated in literature times without number.

The object of Ramón's last great passion was the wife of a Genoese merchant, who had come to Palma. One evening as he rode into the city he saw the lady on her way to evensong at the cathedral. Ramón followed her on horseback right into the church. The lady then approached him and asked him to come to her the same night. Ramón came and was shown into her bedchamber. In silence Doña Antonia listened to his passionate speeches, in silence she began to undress — baring her breasts which Ramón had extolled in his lovesongs; and as he drew back in horror she bade him " Behold." She tore off the blood-stained bandage which covered one breast and forced Ramón to see the cancerous sore which was devouring her white flesh. " O Ramón, thou foolish man — look upon this flesh which thou dost love and desire — see what is its fate. It is corrupt. Often is it corrupted even before we are laid in the grave. Much better hadst thou done if thou hadst bestowed thy love on the only One who is incorruptible, whom thou couldst continue to love for all eternity, Jesus Christ." Ramón went from her as a man who has lost all joy in life. Not long after he gave all he possessed to the poor and retired to a monastery.

This story does not appear in written authorities until fairly late, and Ramón's own account of the events which gave a new direction to his life is far more remarkable.

He was sitting in his chamber one summer evening; all his thoughts were bent upon the mistress with whom he was infatuated at the moment, he was writing a song to her and humming the tune to which he intended to set it. All at once, as he looked up from his parchment, he saw to the right of him Christ on the cross, bleeding in the agony of death. Beside himself with horror, he threw aside his writing materials, flung himself on his bed and buried his face in the pillows.

By next morning he had persuaded himself to believe that the vision was only an image of his fancy and that he had been overtired. He would think no more of it. But a week later he had a sudden feeling that he was not alone in the room. He looked up and saw the same vision. And would not believe. "Neither blows nor punishment, neither pleasure nor endearments, neither the cunning nor the arts of a living person were able to bend or break my will," he says somewhere. The young seneschal was certainly not one who was willing to accept visions. Three times more the silent figure on the cross appeared to Ramón before the knight yielded — and now the Crucified spoke to him: "Ramón, follow Me." Then Ramón turned away from his flighty adventures and his petty worldly ambition, and accepted God's invitation to the mighty adventure and the love that has no bounds.

In his writings Ramón several times refers to the anxieties of this period of revulsion. He was a man of about thirty; it was difficult to rearrange his whole life; he was afraid of ridicule and the incredulous mockery of his friends, when it got about that Ramón had been converted. And he was yet more afraid that it was hopeless for him, with his past, to try to seek love at its source, when he had run wild after its reflections and refractions in all created things. In " The Book of the Lover and the Beloved " we read: " O thou bird, who singest of love, ask my Beloved who has chosen me to be His servant, why He torments me with love. The bird answered: If love did not impose these trials upon thee, how then shouldst thou have proof that thou lovest Him? "

" The Beloved appeared to his lover, clad in new scarlet garments. He spread out His arms to embrace the lover. He bent down His head to kiss the lover. And He remained on high, that the lover might always continue to seek Him."

It would of course be an exaggeration to assert that every single man and woman who is unable to settle contentedly in an erotic relationship, but is continually seeking fresh adventures, may be a potential saint who simply has not found or has refused to obey his or her call. Nevertheless it is not rare, as Christopher Hollis points out in his life of St. Ignatius Loyola, that erotic roving is a particular besetting sin among saints who have not yet grasped what they were made for. The great majority of mankind best learn to love God by loving Him in His creatures, by loving their neighbours. Some few are born to love Love itself in its very source and to fight their way through temptations and the dark nights of the soul to a nearness to God to which ordinary human beings cannot hope to attain until after death, and in this nearness to God their love of their neighbour becomes Godlike — their love of humanity knows no " respect of persons." Who are their father and mother and brothers and sisters and their beloved and their friends? All who seek the Beloved, God — all whom God loves: all.

St. Ignatius with his lyrical infatuation for a lady of the royal house and his prosaic dissipation was unmarried when he discovered his mission. The great Teresa was already a nun at the time when, as she herself confesses, she failed in real love of God and forced her soul to fly low, because no doubt she feared the eagle nature that she felt within her — when she avidly snatched at anything in the shape of diversion, suspecting in herself a terrible power of concentration on the greatest and most dangerous matters. But neither Don Inigo nor Sister Teresa had stored up for themselves and others those elements of conflict which are bound to present themselves when a man or woman marries in spite of having a call to something very different from marriage.

That marriage is a call has always been maintained by the Catholic Church — and the state of being married, without having a call to it, is only a few degrees less terrible than being put into a convent without having a call to the monastic life. Ramón Lull had allowed himself to be married and had brought children into the world in those youthful years when he himself did not suspect why he could not settle down and be a good husband and father.

From the first day of his new life Ramón burns to be

able to devote himself to the Beloved, now that at last he has become what he was born to be, a lover and nothing but a lover. Neither enthusiast nor dreamer, but a man who is just as willing to serve his Beloved by daily drudgery as by knightly deeds. The mystical experience transforms the idler into a man of action. The asceticism he imposes on himself to atone for his sins of physical indulgence make him tough and strong, able to sustain all bodily and spiritual strains and privations. He is become a man of energy and initiative who can bear seeing his plans crossed and his hopes dashed — he may alter them, extend them, look for new methods of realizing them, but he never abandons his object: the greater glorification of the Beloved and the widening of His kingdom.

Never is the Beloved out of Ramón's thoughts — and he longs to be allowed to suffer for his Beloved, who has suffered for him, not only once long ago, but again and again for all men who fly from the love of God or refuse to hear of it. Even at this time Ramón has a secret hope that one day he may be permitted to prove his love by the death of a martyr. But he is willing to work hard and long, with all his faculties, in order to deserve the prize. Ramón's brain teems with plans.

Many thoughtful Christians had abandoned the belief that crusades and wars and violence were the right means of attaining that for which all Christian souls yearned — the conversion of the Mohammedans and Jews. This was in the early 1260's, the interval between St. Louis' disastrous Egyptian campaign and the expedition to Tunis, where he died. Christian garrisons still held with great difficulty Antioch and Acre, Tripoli and a few fortresses here and there in Palestine and Syria — the last remnants of the kingdoms that had been conquered by the first Crusaders. And the cause of their reverses was clear enough to many Christians. Joinville tells us:

Jean l'Ermin, master of the artillery to King Louis, was in Damascus buying material for crossbows. An aged man who was sitting in the bazaar called him apart and asked if he were a Christian. The officer answered yes. The old man then said: "You Christians must hate one another terribly. For I have myself seen your King Baldwin of Jerusalem, who was a leper,[1] defeat Saladin with only three hundred armed men, while Saladin had three thousand. It is on account of your sins that you are now fallen so low that we take you in the open field like wild beasts." And he inquired further of the Frank, which must wound a father's heart the more deeply, to be given a blow in the face by a stranger, or by his own son? "Now you Christians call yourselves the sons of God."

There was nothing new in Ramón's idea of an army of missionaries who were to go out and preach the gospel to the infidels, unarmed and with no protection of troops or fortresses in their rear — simply relying on God's giving their words, lives and deaths the power to work wonders, if they sought nothing but His glory. And of course others before Ramón had understood that such missionaries must know something of the language and mode of life of the countries they were to work in. The

[1] Baldwin the Leper, died 1185.

Dominicans amongst others had taken up the study of oriental languages in several of their convents, partly with the idea of training missionaries. But Ramón considered that these studies would have to be greatly extended and carried on more systematically; separate convents would have to be established with the special object of educating missionaries, and the monks would have to receive thorough instruction not only in the oriental languages; they ought also to acquaint themselves with the real nature of Islam and Judaism and acquire a knowledge not only of their beliefs and doctrine, but of their popular customs and conditions of life. When, a few months after his conversion, Ramón set out on a long pilgrimage, his object was not merely to seek " sundry hallowed places," but also to visit the courts of princes. He intended to avail himself of the connections formed while he was a courtier; for the establishment of these schools for missionaries appeared to be a
•project which the conflicting princes of Europe would unite in supporting. He was absent about two years on this, his first pilgrimage.

In the winter of 1265 he returned to Palma and applied himself to the studies which were to enable him to write his books. For he had long believed that there must exist an " Art General " — a method — whereby the doctrine of Christianity as a whole and in every detail could be presented so convincingly that every man of good will must believe. His first book was a vast work, divided into five books in honour of the five wounds of Christ, and subdivided into forty sections in memory of the forty days' fast in the desert. The book contains three hundred and sixty-six chapters, each divided into ten paragraphs in memory of the ten commandments, and each paragraph is divided into three in honour of the Trinity, and so on. This kind of numerical symbolism was popular in the Middle Ages, and Lull has carried it to extremes in many of his writings. The contents of this *Libre de Contemplació* are diverse: autobiography, political essays, theological expositions and mystical meditations. What is interesting for our time is the clear-sightedness with which Ramón seeks to determine what element there is in Christianity that makes it peculiarly incomprehensible or repellent to Moors and Jews, and how these difficulties create prejudices, leading them to the conviction that Catholics believe and teach things which are totally alien to Catholicism. In the first place there is the doctrine of the Trinity, which the others interpret as teaching that there are three Gods, and the dogma of Christ's incarnation and His pre-existence from eternity. To Lull it is clear that men could not have had any knowledge of God, beyond a general intuition, unless God had taken upon Himself human nature and spoken to men in human language. In general Lull has a pronounced distrust of religious mysticism, when emotion emancipates itself from the paths of thought; emotion is far too liable to be seduced by our own secret wishes and idiosyncrasies. At the same time he attempts in this first work of his to clear away a number of Catholic prejudices and erroneous ideas concerning the aliens' beliefs. Ramón Lull, who was to be known as the apostle of Africa, had already discovered the fundamental principles of his missionary work. The book was written in Arabic, in part at any rate, and afterwards translated into Catalan, Ramón's mother tongue. His private life during these years was surrounded by many difficulties. The year after his return he had sold the greater part of his estates and bestowed the money on hospitals and almshouses. But he was married and a father, and the Church has always maintained that a married man has no right to give away so much as would leave him unable to provide for his family in a way which may be called modest but becoming to the station he and his wife occupy. He who desires to serve Christ in the utmost poverty and homelessness must be free — no one has the right to force others into extreme renunciations and ascetic exercises; all such things are spiritual adventures which must be chosen voluntarily. Ramón, then, had kept enough to enable his wife and children to live more or less as they had been accustomed, and he lived with them. It was to a certain extent the same dilemma as Leo Tolstoy had to face some centuries later. Ramón has told us nothing directly, so far as I know, about his relations with his wife during these years. That at times he felt an almost intolerable longing to give up not only his home life, but even his studies and authorship, to betake himself to the wilderness and live alone without being lonely as he was in his home — of this he makes no secret. But the Church has never permitted a married man to evade the duties of marriage, without his wife's consent. In his novel " Blanquerna " Ramón re-

lates how the hero's father, Evast, proposes to his wife
Aloma, when their son has left home, that they shall both
retire to convents. Gently but resolutely Aloma refuses;
she will gladly consent to her husband giving away all
they possess, turning their house into a hospital for the
poor, and they may well take vows of chastity now that
they are so old; but she insists that he shall remain with
her; poverty, privation and sacrifice she is ready to bear,
but all this they must share in company with one another. Nobody can say whether Doña Blanca looked
upon her husband's changed mode of life in this light,
or whether a marriage such as that of Evast and Aloma
was merely an imagination of Ramón's. A little book on
education which he wrote when his son Dominic was
nearly grown up was perhaps intended as a sort of testament to the boy, who was now to enter upon his own life
as a man, and a justification of the father for the education he had given, or tried to give, his children. But we do
not know how they regarded it, when he who had been
one of the richest and most powerful lords in the country
voluntarily parted with all his superfluous possessions
and brought them up in strict frugality and piety. That
he loved his children and yearned for them and for his
wife during his absence appears from many passages in
his writings — it is one of the motives that often make
him weak and uncertain how to act rightly.

For his own part he could live as a poor man and dress
as a man of the people, spend his day, from the time he
went to Mass in the morning till the late hour when he
put away his books and manuscripts, in constant prayer

and persistent work — he was nevertheless master in his house and master of his wife's servants. He had not yet grown insensitive to the surprise and scoffing of his former friends, to the small town's ridicule of the seneschal who had turned sanctimonious. He had felt inclined to go away for a few years, to study at a university on the mainland. St. Ramón of Pennafort dissuaded him from this; perhaps the great Dominican saw in it a masked attempt at flight on the part of Ramón Lull. And it was his duty to administer what he had retained of the family fortune to the best of his ability. It is clear from the books which he wrote at various times " for his son Dominic " that, while he desired that his children might be called to the life of contemplation, he would not bring any pressure to bear on them — he speaks of the place of prayer in a Christian home, in case they should be married. Magdalena Lull was married. Possibly it was due to her marriage having been arranged and to Dominic's being grown up according to mediæval ideas — the boy may have been about seventeen — that in 1275, after having studied and worked at home for nine years, Ramón at last considered he had the right to seek solitude for a while. He betook himself to a cave on the summit of Mont Randa. In the wilderness his soul was to find rest for a time in unbroken communion with the Beloved.

Legend has embroidered the scanty accounts which Ramón's writings give us of his visions and ecstasies in the hermitage on Mont Randa. There Nature became as an open book to him, " in the trembling of the leaves he

could read of obedience, in the scent of the flowers what
benefits come from suffering and adversity." " A single
day on Mont Randa could teach him more than a year
spent among his books at home, if the Beloved would
make tryst with him there." He himself thought that in
his cave on the mountain he had been directly inspired
from on high as to the plan and writing of his chief work,
Ars Magna. One day, as Ramón was praying in the cave,
the crucified Christ again appeared to His servant and
allowed Ramón to embrace Him — and when Jesus
Himself vanished, He let His cross remain in the arms
of the lover.

From his solitude on the mountain Ramón went to
the Cistercians in the convent of La Real, where he wrote
his book *Ars Magna,* or Art General. He himself firmly
believed the book to be inspired, and always regarded
it as his principal work. It has great historical interest, as
a kind of mediæval encyclopædia of theological specula-
tion and of the natural science of that day. But it is not
among those works of Ramón Lull which speak to us
directly across the intervening centuries, as do his semi-
fictional works, with their fresh and spring-like rudi-
ments of realistic portraiture, their lively episodes and
their radiant joy in the beautiful scenery of his native
land. And only here and there does it show evidence of
kinship with those of his works which are immortal so
long as Christianity exists — the lyrical, ringing beauty
with which Ramón Lull can tell of the love between the
poor and rich human soul and the ever-loving God — in
the book of *Amic e Amat:* the Lover and the Beloved.

Ramón was not destined to return to his home in Palma. After accomplishing the great work of his life among the Cistercians of La Real he wrote a few smaller books, on more popular lines. Then he went back again to his hermitage on the mountain. And from there he moved to Montpellier, to visit his old pupil and master, Prince Jacme. He asked that his writings might be submitted to the censorship of theologians and presented his plans for his great missionary work. King Jacme the Conqueror died the same summer (1276) and his dominions were divided between his sons Pedro and Jacme. Immediately on his accession to the throne of Majorca King Jacme II founded Miramar, a convent in which thirteen Franciscan friars were to be perpetually engaged in the study of Arabic and Hebrew according to Ramón's plans. In his lyrics and in his prose works Ramón constantly returns to this foundation, which gave him the greatest joy of his life. It was a bitter disappointment to him that the college never performed the miracles he had expected of it and ceased to be a house of study in his own lifetime.

3

DURING Ramón's stay at Montpellier his wife had applied to the authorities in Palma and secured the appointment of a relative of hers as administrator of the family property, "since her husband had become so devoted to the contemplative life that he was unfit to attend to their temporal welfare." Thereby Ramón was

4 6

released from his domestic obligations. He was now a man of over forty.

He removed to Miramar. The convent stood by the sea-shore on the north of the island, a little way up the mountain-side, which at that time was covered with a forest of oaks. The neighbourhood is reputed to be the most beautiful in Majorca; in particular the view from Miramar of the sunset over the sea is magnificent. In his account of Blanquerna's life in his hermitage Ramón is believed to be describing his own memories of Miramar.

Every night at midnight Blanquerna rises and opens the window of his cell. With his eyes fixed on the heavens and the stars he begins his prayer " in order that his whole soul might be with God." He prays until daybreak, when the monks go to the convent church, then he accompanies them to Mass. After that he walks on the hills or along the beach, until body and soul are refreshed, and then returns to his studies in his cell. He says his hours at the canonical times like the monks, and after terce he takes a light meal of vegetables and water; afterwards he works in the garden " so as not to give way to indolence and in order to keep his body healthy and able to withstand exertion," until the time of the midday meal. He repairs alone to the church to say the prayer following the meal, and then he sleeps, usually by the fountain in the garden, until sunset. After that he goes up again into the mountain to pray. More often than not he remains awake all night. " And Blanquerna was filled with such great love and passion during his prayers

4 7

that if he fell asleep it seemed to him that he was still
with God, as though in contemplation."

A number of his books were composed in the two
years he spent at Miramar. " The Book of the Heathen
and the Three Wise Men " no doubt received its final
shape here. A philosopher who has no religion sets out
to seek knowledge and comes to a wonderfully beautiful
forest. Beside a spring in this forest he encounters the
three wise men, a Jew, a Christian and a Saracen, to
whom the symbolic meaning of the trees and flowers
and springs is expounded by the beautiful maiden Intelligencia. Each of the three wise men explains his religion to the heathen.

As always Ramón tries to be just. He makes both the
Jew and the Saracen set forth their beliefs with pathos
and feeling. The Jew says, amongst other things: " From
love of God we endure the captivity in which we live,
despised by Christians and Saracens alike. And if God
would not come to the help of us, who might gain
our liberty at any time if only we would abandon the law
under which we live, then His love and His power and
justice could not be perfect — but that is impossible.
And because we know it to be impossible we have a sure
trust that God will send us the promised Messias, who is
to lead us out of captivity." He recalls that his people
has twice before lived in captivity, once for seventy
years and once for four centuries, but this latest exile
will soon have lasted for thirteen hundred years. The
heathen asks if it may not be that a burden of guilt
weighs upon this people, since their misfortunes have

persisted so long, and if the Lord may not be waiting for penance and conversion before He can come to the help of His people?

The words of the Saracen are in great measure taken from the Koran. Again and again emphasis is laid on what the three wise men have in common: the faith in one God, in His omnipotence, goodness and justice, and in an eternal life in which every man shall reap what he has sown during his life on earth. But the Christian, in his belief in God's incarnation and atoning death, the fruits of which He is willing to share with all mankind, has a source of faith, not only in God's goodness and justice, but in His mercy and His tenderness.

In " The Book of the Holy Ghost " the fair maid Intelligencia rides in the same flowery forest and waters her horse at the same spring. This time it is an Orthodox Greek and a Catholic who are reposing on the grass and arguing about the disputed *Filioque* in the confession of faith. Again Ramón tries to understand the standpoint of the other side and to render explicit what unites the two as well as what divides them. Two long poems written at this period, " Our Lady's Sorrows " and " Our Lady's Book of Hours," are full of reminiscences of the lays of the troubadours. The matter of Ramón's verses, like that of innumerable other mediæval poems — among them the Icelandic *Lilja* — consists of the story of the life of Christ and of theological reflections, but every strophe begins or ends with an appeal to the Virgin Mary, who knows all these things better than living men and by her intercession can enlighten the

4 9

poet, so that his knowledge may be extended and his love of God increased.

In 1277 Ramón left Miramar and went to Rome. His object was nothing less than to induce the Pope and the cardinals to establish colleges after the pattern of Miramar over the whole wide world; all that was required was an extension of the study of languages to include all heathen tongues " in order that the whole world might be converted." Pope John XXI was himself one of the great scholars of the age, and he had shown a burning zeal for the missions. Ramón was no doubt aware of this. But when he arrived in Rome the Pope had just died. We do not know why Lull did not stay in the city to await the election of a new pope — only that the state of things in Rome caused him bitter disappointment every time he came there. Ramón vanished, and very little is known for certain of his life during the next five years — only that he set out on a prodigious journey to the uttermost bounds of Christendom, and even beyond. Tradition asserts that he visited England, Denmark, Gotland, the Slavonic countries of the Baltic, " where every man believes he has a god in his field and another in his stable and yet another god in his garden." He was acquainted with the Tatars in Russia, but it cannot be said with any certainty how much of his knowledge was due to personal observation and how much he had gathered from other travellers. He visited Palestine and North Africa, but whether he himself was ever in Abyssinia or among the negro peoples of whom he writes, is uncertain.

Then in 1283 Ramón suddenly appears at Montpellier, where the Dominicans were holding a general chapter. He had formerly been closely connected with the
Order, and he must have assumed that the preaching
friars would enthusiastically associate themselves with
his plans for a world-embracing mission. Instead he met
with a chilly reception at the hands of the learned
monks; they found his " method " amateurish and his
plans fantastic, and reminded him that he was a layman
and self-taught. Ramón never forgave the Dominicans for
this and reproached the Order with lukewarmness. It
retaliated by endeavouring after his death to have his
writings destroyed as being full of heresies; " Lullism,"
the method which the Franciscans had developed on the
basis of Ramón's " Art," was banished from all semi-
naries.

Ramón stayed a couple of years at Montpellier. King
Jacme II was driven from Majorca by his nephew and
retained only Roussillon of all his possessions; meanwhile his former seneschal was studying, giving lectures
and writing his masterpiece, the novel " Blanquerna."
This treats of the aspirations of Ramón Lull's soul — all
he desired to accomplish for the glory of God and the
salvation of men, of his belief that a Christian man who
unconditionally devotes himself to God and fights His
fight with undivided will can work wonders. But he
does not make himself the hero of the story — he intro-
duces himself in the course of it as " Ramón the fool,"
" the fool of Love," he crosses Blanquerna's path casu-
ally, so to speak. But Blanquerna is the pure youth who

has yearned from childhood to be able to live in the stillness and solitude of the woods, to hold unbroken converse with the Beloved in prayer and contemplation. But while journeying through the forests to seek a place where he may build his hermitage he is recalled to active life — one adventure after another befalls him, bringing him to cottages and castles, where tasks are imposed on him which for the sake of God he cannot refuse to accept. He is led to a monastery which is suffering from an invasion of worldly and turbulent guests; Blanquerna converts them, but the monks, who have been infected by the evil spirit, insist that he must remain with them. Blanquerna is made abbot, becoming responsible for the spiritual and temporal welfare of a number of men. The worldly Bishop in whose diocese the monastery is situated comes in conflict with Blanquerna, but is converted — and much against his wish Blanquerna is chosen Bishop in the other's stead and has to take upon himself new and yet more onerous tasks. Ecclesiastical affairs oblige him to go to Rome, and there he is elected Pope. But the man who never refuses to perform the work imposed on him in the service of God converts all who come in contact with him; institutions are reformed, the Church herself is totally regenerated, zealous and courageous armies of missionaries pour out beyond the bounds of Christendom. And finally, towards the close of his life, Blanquerna feels that he may lay aside the tiara and seek repose in a hermitage, where forest and sea and mountain and birds and beasts are the choir which joins in his songs of praise to the Beloved. This section of " Blanquerna " is " The Book of the Lover and the Beloved " — one of the jewels in the religious poetry of all ages.

Ramón himself was nevermore to find an abiding place on earth. He visited Rome again in 1285, making a digression to Bologna, where he renewed his attempts to come to an understanding with the Dominicans. In Pope Honorius IV he found at last support for his plans. The Pope established a missionary college in Rome on the model of Miramar and strove to have others founded in different countries, in Paris amongst other places. Thither went Ramón, no doubt with a papal letter of recommendation to the chancellor of the Paris university. For a year he studied and lectured there, indefatigably writing books which were to hasten the conversion of the world. Nicholas IV became Pope, and Ramón left for Rome, by way of Montpellier, in order to submit his plan for the reconquest of the Holy Land — he had now come round to the belief that a crusade would be necessary in order to establish a base for missionary work, and that it might be successful if only the Christian princes kept the peace among themselves. While he was in Rome the news came that the Christians had lost the last remnant of the realm of " Oultremer." Acre had fallen, in May 1291.

Now Ramón would wait no longer for fellow-workers. He went to Genoa and took passage in a ship which was bound for North Africa. It must be put to the proof whether with his " Art " he could convince the unbelievers of the sacrificial death of the Son of God. But by this time the extraordinary man had become a kind of celebrity; the Genoese hailed him as a saint and a worker of miracles. And Ramón lost heart — he was only a poor sinner. If he ever succeeded in coming ashore in Barbary, the Moors would certainly not listen to him, in any case they would not grant him a free hearing. They would simply stone him or shut him up — and he had so much left to do. He let the ship sail without him. The reaction came immediately; and now it seemed to him that he had refused to give to God what He had asked of him, had shown incredulity and cowardice and scandalized the least of God's little ones with his want of faith. He fell sick with sorrow and remorse, so that those around him thought he would die or lose his reason. Horrible visions tormented him, and in the extremity of his despair Ramón resolved to bow to God's judgment without praying for mercy — he was ready to go to Hell himself, if only God would allow his work to bear fruit in the salvation of other souls. Then he heard that a galley lay in the harbour, ready to sail for Tunis. Sick as he was Ramón had himself carried on board, and no sooner was the ship at sea than Ramón's mystical sufferings vanished and he was filled with uncontrollable joy and intrepidity.

As soon as he arrived at Tunis he daringly went up to the most famous Mohammedan theologians in the town and challenged them to dispute with him — declaring himself willing to become a Mussulman if they could convince him that theirs was the true religion. And he was actually able to bring about a series of public disputations which resulted in his gaining converts, in such numbers as to alarm the caliph, who had him arrested and brought to trial. Ramón was condemned to death, but on the intercession of one of the Moorish theologians his sentence was reduced to banishment. As he was being taken from prison to an Italian ship the excited populace tried to snatch him from his escort to stone him. Bleeding and spat upon he was brought on board, but tried to steal ashore again. He had seen that he *could* win souls for Christ; what then did it matter that death was certain sooner or later, if he stayed in Tunis? Nevertheless he allowed himself to be persuaded that for the moment he could accomplish nothing here. But he knew that he must come back.

The ship put him ashore at Naples. He lectured there, wrote and preached to the Moors, of whom there were many in the city. In the summer of 1294 news came that an ascetic hermit had been elected Pope; and Ramón hastened to Rome, certain that the time of miracles was at hand. His missionary plans were now on a yet wider scale: the conversion of the Tatar peoples was just as important as that of the Saracens and Jews. As yet the greater part of the Mongolian tribes had nothing that could be called religion, and they were willing to change their obscure and oppressive Shamanism for a faith which offered them a richer spiritual life. Christian missionaries were well received among them. But both Jews and Mohammedans were working to convert them to their religions. Ramón's first thought was for the salvation of souls. But he was clear-sighted, and he saw that if all these Asiatic peoples became Mohammedans or Jews it would mean a terrible danger to the whole of Christendom.

If he had met with sufficient comprehension, it may be that the whole world would present a different appearance today. For geographically speaking Europe is not a continent, but merely a peninsula of the Asiatic continent, like India and Farther India. Europe is a spiritual continent, created by the Catholic Church, reaching as far as she was able to spread the gospel that God so loved the world that He gave His only begotten Son in order that not a single soul shall perish except by its own will — and together with the doctrine of the unique and eternal value of every single soul she contributed the inheritance adopted from Hellas and Rome, the ideas of the ancients as to the dignity and worth of the human personality.

But in Rome matters went from bad to worse during the saintly old man's papacy. The miracle that this unworldly anchorite might prove himself a man of action, capable of reducing a turbulent age to order and tranquillity, did not take place. Celestine V abdicated after a reign of a few months, like Blanquerna — only that he had never reigned. His successor was Boniface VIII. Neither with him did Ramón find the support he asked for. He gave expression to his bitterness in a long poem, "Desconort" — which means disconsolateness. Once more Ramón recalls his wild youth, his conversion and his labours for over thirty years to lead men to the Beloved — he can see no result of them. Those who have

power to do so will not help him, they count him a
visionary. Out in a forest he meets a hermit, who com-
forts him like Job's friends, reminds him of all his errors,
and asserts that no man can prove the truths of Christianity by arguments. Ramón protests: he himself has
never held that to be possible; man's limited little understanding cannot grasp the infinite. But the intelligence God has given to men is nevertheless of such value
as to enable them to understand that they ought to be
Christians, serving and loving God. And for himself
Ramón holds that God has given him such discernment
as obliges him to account for the talents entrusted to
him. The hermit consoles him: God is just. He will
surely reward Ramón for all he has attempted in good
faith to accomplish. Ramón exclaims—he knows his
Beloved and loves Him. The hermit bursts into tears,
and he and Ramón fall into each other's arms and kiss
each other.

After completing this poem, which Catalan scholars
regard as linguistically the most beautiful and most
musical of his works, he went to Assisi and was received
as a Tertiary into the Franciscan Order. The Minorites
had long shown him the sympathy which he had looked
for in vain from the Dominicans, and after his death
the Blessed Ramón Lull was accounted one of the Franciscans' holy men. This is no doubt partly responsible
for the legend making a monk of him — Ramón lived
and died a layman. But the literary tradition of the ro-
mantics had often a mere superficial knowledge of
Catholicism: it was notorious that Catholic priests

guarded their privileges jealously. Now the clergymen of the Protestant communities were in the first place preachers and were often very unwilling to tolerate the appearance of lay preachers. It had escaped observation that the priests of the Catholic Church are consecrated to administer the sacraments; preaching was not their first duty as priests — as a matter of fact they often neglected it. The Catholic Church has gladly allowed lay preachers a hearing, except, be it noted, in the centuries immediately following the Renaissance, when the body of eloquent laymen who had been making free with her pulpits seemed to render caution advisable. But St. Francis, for example, was a layman and had originally intended his Order to be a league of lay preachers — a salvation army, if you like: even women lay preachers are to be found among the canonized saints. " Let women keep silence in the churches," so was St. Paul's pronouncement on the matter translated — but that did not prevent St. Hildegard from preaching in the churchyards and market-places of German towns, nor St. Catherine and St. Colomba of Rieti from preaching repentance in papal palaces.

Ramón continued his wanderings and his writing; he was again in Genoa, Montpellier and Paris. At the beginning of the new century he was in Barcelona. King Jacme II had regained possession of Majorca, and Ramón visited his native town, Palma, and preached to the Jews and Arabs of the islands. Then it came to his ears that " the Grand Tatar " had made himself master of the whole of Syria and Palestine. That meant that the leadership of Islam was passing more and more to the Turkish and Tatar races, who were recent converts to Mohammedanism and whose faith was firm, fanatical and puritanical, whereas scepticism and mysticism had been gaining ground in the Arab world. Ramón took ship for the Orient; with a pile of new controversial writings in his baggage he set out to convert the Great Khan and his people. He reached Armenia. And returned to Montpellier. In Lyons he again found a new Pope — Clement V. Once more he travelled to Paris, and there Ramón Lull, now a white-bearded old man, attended the lectures of a young Franciscan from the wild West, Duns Scotus. And suddenly he departed for North Africa.

One fine day he turns up in the market-place of Bugia, near Tunis, crying with a loud voice: " The law of the Christians is holy and true and the doctrine of the Moors is false; this I am ready to prove." A furious mob flung itself upon the old man, and strangely enough they did not kill him on the spot but dragged him before the cadi. Still more remarkable does it appear to us that the cadi is said to have received Lull with a certain degree of goodwill and to have arranged a formal disputation between the Christian and learned Mohammedans. He protected Ramón from a raging mob who wished to stone him, and during all the months of his imprisonment at Bugia Ramón received constant visits from Saracen sages who tried to convert him to Islam. With one of them he made an agreement that they should exchange writings. The result was a book, " Disputa-

tion between Ramón the Christian and Hamar the Saracen." After being deported from Bugia in 1308 he sent
copies of it to the Pope and the cardinals. This time he
points out, amongst other things, that while the Mohammedans, as in his own case, offer eventual converts
every conceivable material advantage, and indeed act
up to their promises to renegades, it is often difficult for
a convert from Islam to Catholicism to obtain the barest
necessary help or to find a grain of charity among his
new co-religionists. This is stupid, besides being un-
christian. Again he draws attention to the danger from
the East — but Christendom was now lacking in worldly
wisdom as well as religious zeal.

On his way from Bugia he suffered shipwreck and
was rescued with difficulty, but lost all his books and
clothing — was put ashore at Pisa, in a wretched state
after his imprisonment and sea voyage. The Dominicans
of the city received him kindly, and in their convent
he at once set to work on several new books. He had now
conceived a plan according to which all the Orders of
knights were to be combined and reorganized, and the
Pisans furnished him with money, letters of recommendation and promises. Ramón set out to find the Pope in
Avignon. Just at this time Clement V had ignomini-
ously submitted to King Philip le Bel and acquiesced
in the proceedings against the late Pope Boniface VIII
and against the Order of Templars; and on the other
hand he joined heart and soul in the plans for the disastrous Crusade of 1310 — he had given ninety thousand
florins to the Knights Hospitallers who were to play a

leading part in it. But when Ramón came with his advice he was thrust aside.

He returned to Paris and lectured, this time to crowded audiences; the University bore him testimony that there was nothing in his teaching and writings that conflicted with the Catholic faith. Here amongst other works he wrote at Christmas time 1311 his tract of " The Birth of the Little Child Jesus ": six fair ladies whose names are Prayer, Praise, Compassion, Penitence, Confession, and Good Deeds, have been persecuted by the World. Sick with sorrow at the injustice and misery among men they have decided to fly to the desert and hide from their pursuers. But Prayer finds a better way — they make a pilgrimage to Bethlehem, find the Child in the manger and worship Him. Each sings her hymn to the Virgin Mary: in her Son they have found Him who can convert the hard hearts of men, and now they know that they are to seek consolation for all their sorrows, not by hiding in the desert, but by serving Jesus with heart-felt devotion.

In the same year Ramón attended the Council of Vienne, seeking once more for acceptance of his ideas about training colleges for missionaries, a new Order of knights, and a campaign against Averroism. In one of his writings at this time he defends himself against those who call him a fanatic and a visionary. Visionary is not the word for one who has spent forty-five years in fighting and working for the extension of God's kingdom, but for all those who fritter away their lives in petty conflicts and the pursuit of beggarly self-interest.

In the following year he went home to Palma. He was nearly eighty years old, but it was not his intention to end his days in peace. On the contrary, he made his will. He gives " his body to the worms and to the dust of the earth, that the winds may blow it about so that no one will remember it any more . . . the longings and desires of his heart and the tears of his eyes to all who love his Beloved and are impelled by love to do penance; to them he also bequeaths his imagination, that it may aid them to picture to themselves the glory of the Beloved and the hideousness of hell. To the Beloved he gives his mind, reason and will. And to all sinners the fear that parted him from the Beloved when he thought of his sins." What little earthly goods he possesses are to be divided among his son, his daughter and son-in-law, the Dominican and Franciscan convents in Palma, some nunneries and poor children. His library and copies of his own works are to be distributed to a number of convents with the provision that the books are to be carefully preserved; they are to be chained to reading-desks and made accessible to all who wish to study them. Having thus put his house in order he set out by way of Sicily on his third and last missionary voyage to Africa.

He landed at Bugia. He hoped no doubt to meet with a martyr's death, but in any case he did not attempt to challenge it: he accepted a letter of protection from his King. Aragon and Tunis had concluded at this time a peace treaty, one of the clauses of which obliged them to grant protection to each other's subjects. From Bugia

Ramón proceeded to Tunis, and from there he wrote to King Jacme asking him to send out a coadjutor, a Franciscan, Fray Simó, who had been his pupil. Fray Simó actually joined him in the following year. Ramón was permitted to carry on his work with remarkable freedom from interference; he associated on terms of mutual respect with learned Moors, they did their best to convert one another by verbal and written argument, and Ramón gained five disciples in these very circles of Tunis intellectuals.

From Tunis he returned westward to Bugia. And one day as he was preaching there in the street a zealous Islamite among the crowd picked up a stone and threw it. Next moment the aged missionary sank to the ground under a hail of stones. The populace was in no mood for a reasoned searching after truth. — That is the only certain information we have of Ramón Lull's last hours. Two merchants from Genoa brought his body home to Palma — this was at the end of the year 1315.

Legend of course has more to say. It tells us that the merchants were lying in the roads and at night they saw a pillar of light on the shore, reaching from earth to heaven. They took the ship's boat, rowed ashore and found Ramón broken and bleeding but still alive. One of the Genoese was called Esteva Colom, and the dying Ramón told him of the land far to the west, beyond the sea, which his soul had traversed while his body lay lifeless during ecstasy. Esteva Colom afterwards confided to his sons what Ramón had revealed, and the tale was handed down in the family, till it reached the ears of a boy named Cristobal Colom. But Ramón Lull breathed his last on the morning the Genoese sighted Majorca.

Many years before he had written, in the book of *Amic e Amat:* " The lover thought upon death and was afraid, until he called to mind the city of his Beloved, to which love and death are gates and entrances." " The birds greeted the dawn with song, and the Beloved who is the dawn awoke. The birds ceased their singing, and in the dawn the lover died for his Beloved."

Some fifty years after Ramón's death a controversy raged about his name; the Franciscans had developed a variety of scholasticism which they called Lullism, and the Inquisition under the Dominican Eymeric wished to have Ramón's writings destroyed as heretical — asserting that they taught that man could arrive at faith through his own power and reason, without the aid of grace. Ramón had certainly not taught this, but rather that reason ought to lead a man to pray for faith as a gift of grace. At this time, however, about a thousand works were in circulation under Lull's name, and this mass of genuine and spurious material naturally contained much which the Inquisition could use against the dead mystic. Ramón's authentic works amount to more than a hundred. Meanwhile Rome did not interfere with the Franciscans' cult of the Blessed Ramón Lull, and Eymeric's successors in the Dominican Order themselves discountenanced the persecution of Ramón's writings.

Popular legend made of this strange self-taught man

a magician and an alchemist, although Ramón had expressly declared his distrust of the alchemy and occultism of the age. At last in our time the movement for reviving Catalan as a literary language has led to his being studied as its first and greatest master — of the power and charm of his style I can of course give no very definite opinion, as I have had to confine myself to reading him in translations and extracts. Professor Allison Peers has published an English translation of " Blanquerna " and separately, in handy little editions, " The Book of the Lover and the Beloved," " The Tree of Love," " The Art of Contemplation " and the fable " The Book of the Beasts." In the foregoing I have used in the main his voluminous biography of Ramón, together with Marius André's life of Lull in the series " Les Saints " — that too contains summaries of his works and translated extracts.

SAINT ANGELA MERICI

A Champion of the Woman's Movement

 A YEAR or two ago I saw in a paper an account of a meeting in which representatives of both Catholic and other women's organizations had taken part. One of the non-Catholic ladies had said something to the effect that she was pleased to see the Catholic women had now progressed so far as to be able to co-operate in social problems with other members of the woman's movement. To which a Catholic lady replied that it was we who had cause to rejoice at non-Catholic women having now progressed so far that we could meet and co-operate with them.

A vast deal can be said — and has been said — about all that the Catholic Church has done for women, or against women, in the days of the early Church and in the Middle Ages and later. An infinite amount of contradictory things may be said, for instance, about the position of woman in the Middle Ages. For the fact is that people who enlarge on this subject as a rule have some preconceived opinion or other about it, and therefore what they are in search of is material that may be used in support of this opinion of theirs. It is the easiest thing in the world to compile enormous collections of misogynic utterances from the works of early and mediæval theologians. According to these woman is the inferior sex, woman is untrustworthy, lascivious, quarrelsome, unspiritual, the seductress who tempts man to sin, and she has been this ever since the days of Eve. It is also easy to compile a corresponding collection of utterances glorifying woman — the strong and courageous woman who answers for her faith with her life, the good woman who is a mother to the poor and a sister to the sick, the bride of Christ and the servant of His poor. One can fill volumes with warnings to men against the temptress — and volumes with exhortations to husbands to be forbearing and faithful to their wives, to show sympathy with her weakness, indulgence to her faults, even those of an unfaithful wife. If we chose to search through worldly literature we could gather up bulky tomes of obscene anecdotes and coarse tales and licentious stories of women. We could collect anthologies of the purest love songs, amatory verses fresh with the breath of spring, ballads of lovers' fidelity till death and of maternal love that is stronger than death, love poems that are refined to the point of extravagance. In short, we can find expressions of every possible conception of the relations between man and woman — except the view that after all there may be no great difference between men and women. In other words, the fact that there are once for all two different sexes was treated in a fundamentally natural way by all ancient Catholic tra-

7 0

dition — even if this fact occasionally bewildered people somewhat in one direction or another, making them
at times rather desperate or wild with indignation,
owing to this business of the two sexes being a source of
everlasting complications in a race that has lost its innocence and with it the good will to act rightly and justly;
at other times a trifle delirious with rapture over all the
adventures and surprises that may await one in a world
whose inhabitants present such remarkable differences
as do men and women. But the people of the Middle
Ages were never crazy enough to try to get round the
difficulties by pretending that men and women do *not*
differ to any appreciable extent.

Of course it is the fact that Christian authors of the
period before the Reformation had little but hatred
and contempt for such women as appear in the capacity
of temptresses, especially when they tempt a man to
break his vows. An age which fully understood, not only
the value of asceticism in itself, but the fact that there
are tasks which claim their man so completely that he is
obliged to impose celibacy on himself in order to discharge his duty satisfactorily — even if he be no mystic
but a practical man of action — could not possibly mus-
ter any respect for what it is now the custom to desig-
nate as " sex appeal." It could not look with indulgence
upon women who exploit what " sex appeal " they possess in order to bend a man's will to their own. The confused state of moral ideas at the present time is in great
measure an after-effect of the puritanism which swept
over Europe like a pestilence — with a morality that

commanded people to pretend they didn't know what they did know. The moral anarchy of our day may be excused, in a certain degree at any rate, on the ground that the puritanical " pretend you don't know " morality often led to disgusting hypocrisy; as a reaction against this hypocrisy there arose not only the natural human demand to become acquainted with one's own nature, but a contention that human beings have the right to be as Nature made them; that which is natural is good.

Primitive Christianity taught on the contrary that the natural human being is *not* good, because he is incomplete: he has thrown away a perfection which mankind was created to possess. Only the grace of God, which does not disturb, but perfects, nature, can make man good, since it makes him complete again. But from this it follows that the Middle Ages could have no sympathy for women who try to entice another person to rest content in his imperfect state — whether she tries to lure a man into an unlawful love intrigue, or whether, in an entirely lawful relation — as wife, mother, sovereign — she encourages a man to be greedy, vindictive, arrogant, covetous, unjust, or to enrich his own flesh and blood and pander to his wife's inordinate desire for riches and luxury at the expense of others. Since as a rule it is men who have the say, we need not be surprised if the preachers of morality fulminate in particular against women's love of finery. Rather might it surprise us that they fulminated as much as they did against the expensive private passions of the men. But in mediæval society there was always someone who never abandoned the fight against the avidity of mankind for wealth and power, against the exploiter, against those who refuse to recognize Christ in the poor and sick. Even in times and places where it looked as if all, great and small, priests and laymen, thought of nothing but snatching what they could and plundering their neighbours, there were always voices that whispered or cried aloud: This is not right, it is sin, it is lack of brotherly love, it is fratricide.

There is however a cardinal point in the whole mediæval view of women which I do not remember to have seen emphasized. It is the demand for administrative talent which was then made on all women who wished to deserve the designation of " a good woman " — that is to say, a strong woman. (Weak woman always means bad woman!) We do not meet with the words " administrative talent," but that is what in reality was demanded — of the wife and of the mother, of the princess, of the women of the nobility and the middle class and the peasantry, of women who lived in the world and of those who had entered a convent. One thing is that mediæval society was an entirely agricultural community, and whatever may be the legal position of women, now or in the future, in practice it will always be found that an agricultural community recognizes how immensely important to the welfare of the race is the contribution of its women, in an entirely different way from anything we find in a nomadic community or one which is predominantly maritime or commercial. This does not necessarily mean that she has an

"easy" or a "good time" according to present-day
ideas, but it does mean that peasants cannot keep their
women in a harem. — There is a proverb which says
that the wife brings more to the farm or out of it in her
apron than the man can cart in or out with a pair of
horses. I do not know how far the proverb dates back,
but its truth has been admitted from of old. But the
Christian housewife had to bear the responsibility for
the welfare not only of those nearest to her — or, we
may say, those nearest to her were not only her husband,
children and kinsfolk; her neighbour meant to the
Christian woman of the Middle Ages all with whom she
came in personal contact, the neighbourhood and above
all its sick and poor, the beggar who came to her door
or stretched out his hand to her as she passed on the
road, the whole congregation belonging to her parish
church, the wayfarer who asked shelter of her, the orphans and childless old people who came within her
cognizance.

If instead of confining ourselves to the sermons and
edifying works of clerical authors we take a book by a
layman — for instance, the book written about 1370 by
the Chevalier de la Tour Landry for his own three
daughters, which was translated into a number of European languages, printed in one edition after another
as soon as the art of printing had been invented, and on
the whole must have passed as the standard work on
the education of young women of noble birth right
down to the Reformation — we are struck in the first
place by the demands which the people of that day con-

sidered they had a right to make on parents and on children. The book has suffered the odd fate of being looked upon as improper, at the time when puritanism was rampant. The Chevalier de La Tour Landry wished to bring up his daughters in piety, chastity, sagacity and kindness, but he had no idea that prudishness had anything to do with virtue. And his educational method consists in great part in telling the girls stories with a moral, for their imitation or as a warning. One or two of the latter are indeed of such a nature that it would scarcely occur even to a fairly broad-minded father in our day to tell them to his daughters. But otherwise the book is a gold mine for those who care to make themselves acquainted with the intimate family life of the fourteenth century.

What is most important to the Chevalier de La Tour Landry is his daughters' religious education. First and last he impresses upon them that they are to love God, truly and sincerely; their piety must not be merely show and habit, their praying must be no thoughtless babbling of prayers, but a concentration of the mind on the mysteries of the faith and a reverential and confiding colloquy with God. But he does not disdain to give them good advice about such a matter as the posture of the body which will make it easier to collect their thoughts and avoid distraction while praying, whether at home or in church. For that matter a calm and dignified demeanour is important at all times, not only in communion with God but also in human intercourse. It is above all from love of God and awe of God that they ought to fear sin — but as a precaution their father includes some examples of the ills that may befall one even in this world, if one deserts the path of virtue. Two or three of the tales are designed to give the girls special injunctions to offer many prayers for the dead — not merely for their own dead, but for all the poor souls for whom no one else prays. Now all of us have heard ever since our schooldays a great deal about the income the Church derived from the belief in intercession and how the Catholic clergy exploited this belief and got people to appoint Masses to be said for the souls in Purgatory. The conviction that the living can help the dead manifested itself in other ways of which we do not hear so much — the daily prayer during Mass for all the dead, All Souls' Day (which has now been revived in some sort even in Protestant circles, though there it takes the form of a remembrance of dead relatives in particular). It was not uncommon in the Middle Ages for Bishops, for example, to found daily Masses for all dead persons for whose souls their family had made no such provision. An Icelandic tale relates how a ghost appeared at a banquet to thank the company for concluding its grace with a *De Profundis* for the souls in Purgatory. La Tour Landry tells two stories — actually, no doubt, two variants of the same story — of a girl who had been in the habit of praying for the dead whenever she woke during the night. According to one version she afterwards fell so violently in love with a man as to forget her virtue and honour — according to the other she had to fly and hide from a ravisher. In both versions we are told that when the man tries to seize hold of the girl, he sees a host of spectres forming a guard about her — these are souls from Purgatory who have been released to defend their benefactress.

There is however no sanctimoniousness about the chevalier's religion. His daughters are to show their faith in active kindness and care for their fellow-creatures. He takes it for granted that some day they will be married and will pass their lives in the station to which he himself has been accustomed. He urges upon them that a woman of birth shows her husband respect and obedience — she never contradicts him in the hearing of others, never speaks of him unkindly or disparagingly, but she not only may, she *must* bring him to reason and remind him of his duty and honour in case of need. She is to speak to him in this way when they are alone; and she must do her duty and speak to him as his own conscience, even if her husband refuses to listen — even if he threatens to beat her and drive her away a gentlewoman must not allow herself to be frightened out of saying what is right and true.

The Chevalier de La Tour Landry advises his daughters to take good care of their youth and of their beauty — not after the manner of the ungodly women who paint their faces and dye their hair and pluck out their eyebrows; it is a great sin to try to improve what God has done well and beautifully. Moderation in eating and drinking keeps the figure slim and the complexion healthy. And he tells a cautionary story about a young beauty who received a potential suitor, dressed only in

7 7

a tight-fitting silken kirtle with nothing underneath it — and this was in the depth of winter. And the suitor thought the fair damsel was ugly as sin, with her mildewed grey cheeks and her red nose and blue lips — but her younger sister who had formed no expectations sat there, fresh and red as a rose, for she had prudently put on woollen underclothing, a fur-lined kirtle and a fur-trimmed cape, and so the choice fell upon her. There is something in this piece of paternal edification which applies to all ages. — His daughters are free to deck themselves as bravely as befits their station. But let them not forget the story of the knight's lady who thought of nothing but adorning and dressing up her own mortal body — not one but ten sumptuous gowns did she possess, and each of them had cost enough to keep a poor family for a whole year. When she was dead and her soul was to be weighed in St. Michael's scales, the devil came up, dragging her wardrobe, and emptied the whole contents into the other scale — and so the lady was weighed and found wanting. And let them not do as the other lady who wore her best clothes when she went to a banquet and when she received her kinsfolk and friends — but when she went to church to receive the King of Kings she thought her second-best gown quite good enough. A Christian woman adorns herself above all when she goes to church. — Their father tells them another story of a lady who had two little lap-dogs which she fussed over all day long, bathing them and brushing them and getting them dishes of dainties — although a monk who saw this reminded her that there were poor children in plenty whom she might have cared for instead. But when the lady lay dying, those who stood around her bed saw two little black dogs come and jump up on her, licking her face — and where they had licked the skin turned black, as though scorched. But when Queen Blanche of Castile lay at the point of death, all who were in the room saw that it was filled with tiny shining forms of children. For this energetic lady, the mother of St. Louis, who had ruled France during her son's minority and continued afterwards to take an extremely important part in politics, had nevertheless always managed to find time to attend to the poor and sick, and had made it her special care to succour poor infants, cherishing them like the tenderest of mothers. For this reason a swarm of holy innocents came down from Heaven and bore among them the Queen's soul, when she expired, up to the judgment-seat of God.

The substance of all the stories which the good gentleman relates to his daughters is then that life is responsibility: wealth is responsibility, noble birth is responsibility, power is responsibility, marriage is responsibility — all the circumstances of life demand order, self-discipline, courage, insight and discretion, industry. And only through a right, living relation to God can men gain strength to live rightly. Assuredly the chevalier's positive exhortations form a weighty commentary to the admonitions of the books of homilies: the frivolous, erotic, dress-loving, loquacious, intriguing woman against whom they fulminate could by no possibility meet the demands which that age made on a Christian wife and a Christian man's helpmate.

But the girl who chooses the cloistered life — or who is put into a nunnery — may also be faced with tasks demanding administrative capability and a talent for organization. We have all heard about the great wealth that was gradually amassed by the convents — amongst other reasons because property once bestowed on a convent remained in the possession of that convent, whereas estates in secular hands were continually passing from one ownership to another by division of inheritance and marriage settlement and sale and bargain and seizure. But in addition to the rich convents there were numbers of relatively poor and absolutely poor ones. Especially among nunneries there were many which were anything but rich. For people were seldom prompted to give property to a nunnery by the secret motive, which would often induce a nobleman to show generosity towards a powerful Order of monks, that it might prove a good thing even in this world to have friends in that quarter. And gifts of property to the convents were often subject to clauses obliging the house to feed, clothe and grant pecuniary aid to a certain number of poor people annually. From convent accounts and from reports — from England, for instance, when Henry VIII plundered the convents — we can see that an abbess or a prioress often accomplished almost incredible things in the way of satisfying many mouths with small means. And in fact the evidence from the English nunneries — not that which was made public and has kept alive the legend about the general depravity of the convents, but that which has lain among the archives and has been printed in more recent years — constantly speaks of this or that abbess as " a pious, earnest nun and — a good housewife."

But although it is the case that anyone who contends that in the Catholic mediæval civilization of Europe woman was on the whole reckoned as the second — not the first — sex, can support his view by examples which appear conclusive, yet it is equally certain that women who in one way or another possessed more than average ability were given a chance of developing their talents and exercising them with a freedom from interference which would be inconceivable in a society moulded by Lutheranism or Calvinism. Both the one-sided Lutheran eulogy of a snug family life and the Calvinistic hatred of spiritual charm, of the imaginative and poetical element in religion, and especially the Calvinists' glorification of the industrious accumulation of capital and their belief in economic success as a peculiar favour bestowed on God's elect — all this resulted in a contempt for specially feminine intellectual qualities: intuition, a psychological sense manifesting itself in tact and a gentle dignity in the courtesies of life, discretion and feeling in the work of Christian charity. It is characteristic that when Florence Nightingale was seized with the desire of rehabilitating the nursing of the sick as a work of charity — after it had been for centuries a means of livelihood for bibulous watchers, often superannuated prostitutes, the type of nurse that Dickens

has immortalized under the name of Sarah Gamp —
Miss Nightingale wrote to the future Cardinal Man-
ning, asking him to get her accepted as a pupil in
one or other of the Irish congregations of Sisters of
Charity.

No doubt the movement which rightly or wrongly we
have learnt to call the emancipation of women is in the
first place a result of the transformation of society into
a capitalist and industrial community, in which the
home has lost its importance as an economic and produc-
tive unity. But the bitter tone of the champions of
Woman's Rights in their arraignment of man's rule, the
suspiciousness which refused to believe that anything
but oppression and masculine tyranny was at the bottom
of a great number of laws and customs, which in reality
were designed just as much to safeguard women and
provide them with protectors and maintenance — the
rabidity of militant feminists, in short — was a direct
reaction against a dressing-gown and slippers tyranny
which was peculiar to non-Catholic Europe at the beginning of the nineteenth century — a revolt against
mock heroes who slouched about their homes trying to
assert authority over their womenfolk.

The other day I came across a book which illustrates
in a rather droll way the extent to which Northern European women have taken it for granted that this peculiar North European form of the subjection of women
since the Reformation was characteristic of the whole
past of Europe. It was a little essay by an English writer,
Virginia Woolf — I confess that it is all I have read of

hers,[1] but she is said to have a great reputation as a
novelist. " A Room of One's Own " she calls it, and it
tells of a visit to one of the old English universities.
And she draws a comparison between the wealth of these
universities, resulting from the liberality and cultural
interest of generations, and the unsightly poverty of the
new little women's college. And in searching for the
reason of women having made so small a contribution
to art and science she believes it to be due to the conditions of life with which woman has always had to be
content — not even a room of her own in which to study
or work have the men ever been willing to grant her.
And she indulges her fancy as to the tragical fate which
must have awaited Shakespeare's sister, if she had had
her brother's genius — since society was never disposed
to tolerate, much less encourage the woman of genius.

To our minds it is really odd to see how entirely Miss
Woolf leaves the Catholic tradition out of account. She
thinks that woman makes her entry into the history of
English literature with Aphra Behn, a lady of rather
doubtful reputation who, amongst other things, acted
as a spy under Charles II; she wrote a great many novels
and plays and had considerable talent. Curiously enough
Miss Woolf seems to have forgotten the two English
women writers of the Middle Ages who made important contributions to mystical religious literature. Only

---

[1] Since this was written I have read a good deal of Virginia Woolf.
That she is not only an extremely interesting and talented author, but
an artist of high rank, is one of the greatest literary surprises I have
met with. After " A Room of One's Own " I am bound to say I had expected something very different.

fragments survive — enchanting fragments they are —
of the work of Margery Kemp of Lynn; but Julian of
Norwich's Revelations of the Divine Love is accounted
one of the pearls in all mediæval religious literature, and
there has been no lack of recent editions of the book —
I myself have three that have been published in the last
twenty years — nor of works about Julian and studies
of her personality and her work and her relation to the
religious and philosophic thought of her age.

For the fact is that, so long as Catholicism was the
dominating element in the intellectual life of Europe, a
woman who really had a contribution to make to the
spiritual life of her time was given an opportunity to
do so. Even such spheres of work as in general were
looked upon as the property of men were not closed to
those women who really had the power to accomplish
something in them. People did not exactly expect to
find such qualities in women every day, but if a woman
possessed unusual gifts nobody thought her unwomanly
on that account; she was merely considered to be an
unusual woman. The Apostles themselves perceived
that Our Lord treated women as of the same value if
not the same nature as men, and it is clear enough from
their epistles that in the earliest Christian congregations
the women had their special tasks which were as important as those of the men for the welfare of the whole
body. Women were excluded from the priesthood, because, amongst other reasons, the priesthood has a side
which is turned outwards to the community. A woman
has never been able to become a priest — she cannot

even be a deacon, nor yet a chorister — but a woman can
with the authority of the spirit reprove a priest who falls
short of the dignity of his office, even if his office be that
of the Vicar of Christ on earth. A widow from an outpost
of the Europe of her day — St. Bridget of Sweden — or
a dyer's daughter from Siena, St. Catherine — they bow
humbly before the dignity with which the man is in-
vested, while at the same time speaking their minds
mercilessly and unafraid to the human side of him who
has proved himself unworthy of his vicarship; and they
do this by virtue of the spiritual authority they possess
as favoured souls and as courageous souls. To us Catholics there is no contradiction in this; we know that the
Vicar of Christ is neither more nor less than the Vicar of
Christ. He whose Vicar he is has promised to watch over
His Church so that the gates of Hell shall never prevail
against it. But the Vicar himself is and remains a man
and like all other men can sanctify or desecrate his own
soul; he has his own terrible responsibility, like the rest
of us, only that his responsibility may be said to be
greater on account of the position to which he has been
appointed, above us all.

There has never existed within the Church any prescriptive prejudice against women acquiring all the
learning they could assimilate. And wherever a woman
could really accomplish something of value in the sphere
of scholarship her contribution was received with gratitude and admiration. Even old St. Jerome, who is always being quoted for having said some nasty things
about women — more definitely, about women who

make use of their " sex appeal " — actually collaborated with women for a great part of his life — but, be it noted, with like-minded women who, to put it mildly, were serious ladies. That he happened to take up the work of revising the Latin translations of the Bible was due, to a certain extent at any rate, to St. Paula in the first place. She was a Roman widow who had joined a number of other women in forming a cloistered community. Now she and her nuns complained that the Church's holy scriptures existed in Latin in so many different and divergent translations, and that a number of them must contain sheer copyists' errors, since they were sometimes obviously corrupt and often quite meaningless. When St. Jerome then undertook the translation of the whole Bible, he was assisted in many ways as regards the New Testament by the highly cultivated Roman ladies, St. Paula and her daughter Eustochium — and the Church has never been ashamed of the fact that two women contributed to the production of her biblical classic, the Vulgate.

It was, by the way, the same gruff old Father who wrote some perfectly charming letters to St. Paula's son about the education of his little four-year-old daughter. Amongst other things he advises the father to provide wooden or ivory blocks inscribed with the letters of the alphabet, so that little Paula may learn her letters like a game, and afterwards she can play at putting together words and sentences. Engrave the characters very lightly on the wax tablets and let the child trace them more deeply, with someone to hold her hand until she has learnt to use the style herself. Do not make her lessons too long; little children are as a rule apt to learn, and it is the fault of their elders that they are so often restive and lazy at school — their teachers make them work so long at a time that they become exhausted and lose heart. When she grows a little older her father must see that she is taught Greek; and as a beginning she must be made familiar with the rhythm of the Greek language. But she must also learn her own mother-tongue, Latin, thoroughly and that at an early age; otherwise she will get into the way of speaking it with an ugly accent and misusing it from slovenliness. — The old desert Fathers were neither severe nor inhuman in the demands they made — on other people, who had never professed to have a call for the life of an anchorite or ascetic.

There is no hint of anyone having thought Roswitha of Gandersheim unwomanly for being the first to attempt the writing of Christian Latin dramas — some thing to take the place of the pagan and by no means moral comedies of Terence in the curriculum of convent schools. This Saxon nun who lived in a remote age had probably no other object than breaking new ground in education; she was a poet, and there are scenes and dialogues in her dramas, based on lives of the saints, which move us today — with their freshness and warmth and their knowledge of the human mind and heart. Roswitha, by the way, also wrote historical poems in Latin: the history of her convent and an epic of the Emperor Otto I.

St. Hildegard of Bingen was honoured in her life-

time by others besides her nuns, who worshipped her as
the ideal Mother Superior. Her enormous correspondence shows that princes and prelates, laymen and religious, men and women, all the celebrities of her time
and shoals of nameless people of all classes applied to
the Abbess of Rupertsberg with requests for advice and
inquiries about everything that concerned their spiritual and physical welfare. Visionary, preacher — the
old nun actually undertook missionary journeys and addressed the people in the squares and market-places of
Rhenish and Franconian towns — physician, naturalist
as scientific as it was possible for her to be with the
knowledge of the twelfth century, author of homilies,
anatomical and botanical works, theological expositions,
biographies of saints and dramatic poems — it was to
this German nun that the Popes wrote, begging her to
give them encouragement, advice and her blessing. On
her death in 1179, at the age of nearly eighty, the convent she had built on the bare Rupertsberg near Bingen
was famous all over Christendom as much for the perfect life of its nuns as for its wonderful gardens, for the
model farming and viticulture that was practised on its
land, and for its library, which was one of the largest
north of the Alps.

St. Gertrude, St. Mechtild of Magdeburg and St.
Mechtild of Hakeborn are probably known to most
Catholics, at any rate by name. They are sufficiently
near to us today for their prayers to be found in most
of our prayer-books and their writings to be published
with scholarly commentaries and reprinted without such

apparatus as books of edification for the general body
of believers. I have already mentioned Bridget, Catherine of Siena and Julian of Norwich. Quite apart from
what they signify to us, their fellow-believers, all three
are among the great names of the world's literature. As
a prose author St. Bridget stands by the side of Strind-
berg in Swedish literature; Catherine's mastery in the
treatment of the Italian language has been lauded to the
skies by non-Catholics just as much as by Catholics, and
enthusiasm for Mother Julian's book as an artistic
achievement is specially lively in circles which assume
her faith to be dreams and poetry.

I could go on citing endless examples of women's
contribution to the literature of Catholic Europe — in
Italy, in Germany, in Switzerland, in France. In conclusion I will only mention the greatest of them all —
St. Teresa, to whom Rome gave the rank of doctor ec-
clesiæ and whom Harald Höffding has called a pioneer
of modern psychology.

What made it possible for all these women to develop
and make free use of their peculiar and unusual gifts
was, however, the fact that they lived in a world in
which women were encouraged to cultivate what talents they had. If they could read and write, and that ex-
cellently, this implies of course that women who had
learnt to read and write were no rarities — that they
were surrounded by women and men who shared the
same intellectual life in some degree. The necessary
condition for the lively correspondence between the
nuns and their spiritual leaders was the recognition of

a sphere in which men and women could meet as human beings of equal value; the belief that in the sight of God a masculine soul and a feminine soul were equally precious, alike of such eternal value as to deserve His imparting Himself to them and forming them — but a masculine soul was a masculine soul and a feminine soul was a feminine soul. The differences and variations were a part of the diversity with which the Creator had adorned His creation.

2

For centuries Giovanni Merici's ancestors had lived as peasant proprietors in the neighbourhood of Lake Garda. There had been fluctuations in the family prosperity — crop failures, epidemics, war and invasions made the life of the mediæval peasant insecure, and especially that of the peasants in the northernmost part of Italy on the shores of the beautiful lakes, at the foot of the snow-crowned wall of the Alps. But the Mericis had always been free men, industrious, honourable, stout-hearted men who set to work sowing and planting their land again, every time the country had been ravaged by swarms of grasshoppers or armies from Germany or France.

The old farm-house in which Angela Merici was born on the first of March 1474 still stands by Lake Garda, a short distance outside the little town of Dezensano. She was the fifth child that Donna Merici bore to her husband Giovanni. The sons were the eldest, but they died at an early age, so it comes about that Angela mentions most frequently a slightly elder sister in the recollections of her childhood which she afterwards related to her most intimate friends and which have come down to us in the earliest lives of St. Angela Merici.

Her childhood at home on the farm appeared to Angela in after life as though swathed in a haze of happiness and affection. The love of their parents enclosed the two little girls in its protecting warmth, and over father and mother and the child's whole world there was the loving and almighty God, bending down to screen them as with powerful wings. What Angela remembered was the morning prayer: her father and mother kneeling on the stone floor of the great kitchen — and outside the open door the pale grey morning mist from the lake drifts among the elms which support the trailing vines. The cart is waiting outside, harnessed with great white oxen — Giovanni is going to the fair at Dezensano. Her mother goes about her domestic duties. About midday, when the sound of bells floats in the warm sunny air, the men come home to take a siesta — except in the busiest time, when Donna Merici and her maids have to carry food and drink to them out in the fields, and Angela is allowed to go too, running along the road between hedges and stone walls where the leaves are beginning to look dusty and faded and the green lizards sun themselves. In the evening the fire blazes on the hearth in the great kitchen, and Giovanni reads aloud to his household, from the holy scriptures, from the

lives of saints and from the great book about the life of
the desert Fathers which made a particular impression
on Angela and her sister.

From the roof-beams hung shining hams and thick
black sausages to be smoked. No doubt the whole house
was pervaded by the scent of Giovanni's butt of wine,
blending with the fragrance of the mistress's baking. So
perhaps it was not so strange that, when Merici's little
girls thought they too would show by their acts that they
loved God and wished to make a sacrifice for His sake,
fasting was the first thing that came into their minds.
Respect for food, as a loan from God, and delight in
good food, are deeply rooted in most peasants, and in
none more than Italian peasants. And Catholic asceticism has never taught that we are to renounce the good
things of this world because they are not good — it is
we who are not good. Food *is* a loan from God, wine *is*
a blessing from God — and men make hogs of themselves, gorging without giving thanks and drinking till
their wits, the noblest of God's gifts to men, are fuddled
— when the two pious little girls thought upon this they
could not help being sad and full of shame; they would
do penance, pray and fast, not only on account of their
own little sins, but for all the sinners they saw around
them. It was still half play: at the bottom of the garden,
under some old vines, Angela and her sister had their
playroom, and they played at being anchorites who
were to become saints. *Halb Kinderspiele, halb Gott im
Herzen* —. When Angela was seven her parents discovered that she was in the habit of getting up at night to

pray, kneeling on the cold stone floor. Her father praised her for it, but said she must not do it any more — it was not good for her at her age. And the parish priest came and gave her father his approval — Angela must not practise such exercises — just yet.

People who live in the Protestant tradition have been greatly taken with the fancy that the worship of saints is really nothing but masked polytheism — the saints are the old local divinities of popular belief smeared over with a little Christianity, but they are the same ancient idols with just the necessary coat of paint. So that it is difficult at times even for those of us Catholics who are converts from a Protestant environment to have a complete understanding of what the cult of saints actually is. We know of course that the whole point is, the saints are not gods and never have been gods; even if they have often moved into temples which old pagan gods have had to evacuate, and even if they have often been smeared over with a little ancient paganism, the most ignorant and simple Catholics have always known that they are the very opposite of gods, men — that is, creatures, not creators. Even the most free-handed miracle-workers among the saints do not operate by powers of their own, but by virtue of their association with God who created them and us all. And if popular legend often has a tendency to transform them, making it appear that they were distinguished from birth in a particular way, that from the very first they were equipped with extraordinary and unconventional qualities, this may be due to an unconscious attempt to provide an excuse for us ordinary people, who would be glad to evade the troublesome duty of becoming saints. For that is what all of us ought to be: " Be you perfect, as your heavenly Father is perfect." But when we hear it said of a William Doyle or a Therese Martin that they talked about intending to be saints, as other young people talk about choosing a career or making a good match — we are rather taken aback and inclined to think it a little presumptuous. The longing for sanctification may of course be awakened in a soul in other ways too, but very often it will be seen that a saint found his way to God by following in the footsteps of those who had gone before.

This was Angela's way. Christianity was the very air she breathed. She was born into the Church, as one is born in one's native country; the stories of the saints were the history of her country, the saints themselves its heroes. As is the way of a warm-hearted and high-minded child she began by weaving dreams and fancies about the great men of her people — " worshipping " them in the sense in which a child of our time " worships " a Nansen or an Amundsen; and as she grew up Angela outgrew this childish enthusiasm and attained to conscious self-education: she too would serve her Lord and work in the service of her King, as the holy ones had done before her. At the age of twelve or thirteen she had already made such progress as to discover how her childlike faith became more actual, warmer, richer and more fervent, in proportion as she strove to live according to the teaching of Christ. The more sacrifices she could make, small and great, the more she gained control over herself, the greater was the happiness and reality with which she felt the proximity of God, felt His love enfolding her, even nearer, more intense, closer than the love of her parents. And the love that prevailed between parents and children, between her and her sisters, was in itself a thing wonderfully rich and tender and warm in Giovanni Marici's home.

They were a happy family, and the young girl could still lead a full life in the company of her dear ones. Church festivals and popular festivals — they were all one in those parts, where every feast day began with Mass in the church and was continued in the festive meal after the service, when the whole congregation, who had come to church fasting, sat down in the shadow of the house of God and applied themselves to their baskets and flasks, exchanging food and drinking to one another. Harvest and vintage festivals, processions and mystery plays on the great holidays of the Christian year — Angela attended all these with her parents. They took her to Dezensano and to Salò, the home of her mother's family; she enjoyed it all, but beneath her youthful delight there was a latent presentiment of a deeper, fuller joy — a love which would demand she knew not how much of her, but however much it might be, she knew she was willing to give it all.

" Oh, Angela — what lovely hair you have," said a girl friend to her one day, drawing her fingers through Angela Merici's heavy golden tresses; " it will bring you a fine suitor one day. You are sure to get on in the world."

And the girl herself realized that she had already known for some time in her inmost soul that this was not the way for her. To make a good match — to get on in the world. No, she was not meant to marry. Of course she knew very well that she was good-looking. Golden hair has always been regarded by the Italians as an exceptional beauty. The death mask which was taken of the old, toothless Mother Angela still shows her broad, low forehead, with spacious, finely arched eye-sockets, her straight nose and powerful chin — the sturdy North Italian Juno-like popular type which is known to us from Mantegna's paintings of the Madonna. The fame of her radiant beauty in youth constantly recurs in the oldest biographies. — And now it struck her with dismay: would her fair looks prove an obstacle, preventing her from following the call she had just heard in her heart? Angela surreptitiously scraped soot from the chimney, stirred it up in boiling water and washed her hair in the black mixture to take away its golden gleam.

She was thirteen when she was allowed to receive the holy communion for the first time. To Angela this was the consummation of all that had been growing within her during her childhood. Her parents saw and understood that their second daughter was in some way elect, that she was living a mystical life in the love of God. Donna Merici was anxious at times — especially as Angela, whenever she had been to communion, seemed able to live without food for a whole week. " Now wait, and we shall see," said Giovanni Merici. And their parish priest said the same: time would show what God intended with Angela Merici.

Then her father died, when she was fifteen. Donna Merici submitted piously to the will of God; but it seemed as if the sturdy peasant woman had lost her strength. She tried to carry on her work as before, managing the farm and the house, but it was too much for her. The two elder daughters had to take it up. And Angela, the mystical bride of God, proved to be a capable mistress of a farm, provident and practical; she had the skill and the strength and the ability to arrange and organize the work of others.

Then she lost her elder sister. For a while it was as though Angela was quite paralysed by her grief. Till one day she had to go out with a meal for some of their men who were working in a field a good way from the farm. A little chapel stood by the roadside, and Angela stopped and knelt down for a moment's prayer. And suddenly it was as though she were enveloped in a flood of celestial light — within this light she saw her dead sister and about her a shining host of maidenly forms, and a voice addressed the sorrowing girl in audible words full of consolation and wisdom.

Not long after her mother also died. Angela and a younger sister,[1] a little girl, the only one she had left, went to live with their uncle at Salò. Here they were in

---

[1] According to one of the earliest biographies this child was a little brother who died at the age of nine. For this period of Angela's life her biographers had no authority beyond the few particulars she gave them many years later.

totally different surroundings; the uncle, Signor Biancosi, was a rich man, a man of influence as things went
in the little town. There were no sharp dividing lines
between the peasant freeholders, the well-to-do burghers
who competed for power in the small self-governing
Italian cities and the petty nobility of the surrounding
district. In her uncle's house Angela became acquainted,
on a small-town scale of course, with the festive, colour-
ful, noisy life of the Italian Renaissance — while mutual
strife among the burghers, party quarrels, family conflicts, legitimate and illegitimate love affairs, poverty,
sickness and epidemics, gaming and duelling, swindling
and fraud, luxury and frivolity whirled past the eyes of
the young peasant girl. For a time she did her best to
take part in this life, as her uncle and cousins wished
her to do.

And then one fine day, or rather night, the two Merici
girls disappeared. Angela and her sister had come to the
conclusion that they could never settle down to this life,
and so they had taken the road — home to the paternal
farm and to the anchorites' huts of their childhood
among the trees. But this time they meant it in earnest;
they would dedicate themselves to God and live as
recluses.

Their uncle came after them and brought them back
— with gentle and sensible words, as Angela herself related in after days. He neither scolded nor laughed at
her, but spoke seriously to Angela about the dangers
which threatened a young maid and a little girl alone
in a cabin by the roadside. Angela saw that he was right,

and that she was responsible for her little sister. Subsequent events were to prove that Angela's call was to a very different life from that of a recluse, but as yet she had no suspicion of this — all she understood was that her immediate duty was obedience to her uncle. He promised for his part that his nieces should be left in peace to lead their religious life as they pleased in his home. In return for this Angela took up the work of the house with a will — washing and keeping the linen cupboards, spinning, weaving and sewing, baking, cooking and cleaning. " In so doing the two sisters preached," says the bull of canonization with sound mediæval sense, " as they could never have done in the desert."

These years in her uncle's house matured Angela into a grown-up woman. It was during this time that she made acquaintance with the world she lived in — the world of Alexander Borgia and of the Sforzas, a time of war, the palmy days of political intrigue, the age of religious apostasy and the revival of paganism, but at the same time an age which witnessed the rising of saints in revolt against neo-paganism. She must have heard of Savonarola's conflict and triumph, of his fall and death. Of threats of war and of the Turkish peril, of catastrophes of nature and of the appearance of new and sinister diseases which spread from one country to another, Angela must have heard during these years.

And she learnt to know herself. She learnt to know temptation — the temptations of the world, the temptations of her own strong and ardent nature. She herself afterwards gave an account of the struggles of these years

9 9

and of the wonderful rescue which answered her outcry to God: " Suffer me not to part from Thee."

When Angela was twenty-three the little sister died, to whom she had been both a mother and a sister. Some time after this she obtained her uncle's consent to a plan that had been in her mind: she wished to return to her father's house and live there with a woman friend, to carry on the farm and devote herself to a life of spiritual exercises and services of charity — feeding and clothing the poor, nursing the sick, visiting those in sorrow. That she was called to undertake a task that was to be her own, to begin a new work, was still unknown to Angela at that time.

3

SOME years after her return to the farm at Dezensano Angela Merici entered the Third Order of St. Francis. Thereby she acquired a framework for her religious existence, a life of stated duties towards the living and the dead. She had dedicated herself to voluntary poverty, so she gave away all her possessions, keeping only a single room in the main building of the farm, where she lived in company with her friend. The two women lived on alms which people gave them. When they had nothing else they ate the chestnuts that had fallen from the trees or wild salads that they picked in the fields. From this time on people began to talk about Angela Merici's cheerful nature — her radiant humour, her witty and whimsical repartees which were repeated far

and wide — and they came from great distances to ask
her advice alike in spiritual difficulties and practical
affairs. Young girls began to gather round la donzella
Merici, who according to the ideas of that time was becoming an old maid.

Angela discovered that she had quite lost her call to
forsake the world. She felt that a convent was no home
for her. But what then? For she knew at the same time
that Christ had called her to Him in order that she
should be His alone, His own bride. But to be a nun
without a convent — that must have seemed to all her
friends and even to herself a strange idea, almost an
abnormal one. And she knelt through long nights of
watching, praying and asking: " Lord, what wilt Thou
have me to do? " War brought sickness and distress to
her native district, day after day Angela had enough to
do and more than enough, but when late in the evening
she came back to her little room in the old farm-house,
the question was there again, bringing its feeling of
unrest and anxiety, uncertainty and expectation.

Then the friend with whom she had been living also
died. Angela felt her loss deeply — and to her sense of
loneliness and of her life being so out of the common
that it could not possibly be right was added the presentiment that there was something which she had to
accomplish, but she could not find out what it was.
Then there came a day when Angela was walking with
a troop of girls on a path beside the lake. She had stayed
behind her companions, kneeling in the shade of some
great trees — Brudazzo is the name of the place where

tradition says St. Angela had the vision which she herself regarded as one of the decisive experiences of her
life. A vision of celestial light, like that she had seen before, but this time much clearer and more unearthly, as
it were shining tones flowing over her and raising her
up from the ground on waves of flame and sound; and
then she saw a ladder between earth and heaven, and
up and down this ladder passed singing virgins clad in
white with crowns of radiance on their heads. One of
them detached herself from the rest, her dead friend,
and she spoke to Angela:

"You must know, Angela, that God sends you this
vision to tell you that before you die you will have
founded a company in Brescia, a company of virgins
such as these."

A company — that is a technical military expression.
When St. Ignatius founded the Order of Jesuits he called
it at first the Company of Jesus. It does not appear that
Angela Merici ever found anything to wonder at in her
being called to enrol a company and presumably to lead
it as long as she lived — in her being appointed an officer in the Church militant. In reality we may be sure
that the people of the Middle Ages took a more natural
and straightforward view of such a phenomenon as a
woman occupying a position of leadership — there was
no political implication compelling women to show that
they *can* be leaders. The assumption was that it is best
for people in leading positions to be exceptional persons. It is rarer to find women who are born to be lead-

ers; but since it is a notorious fact that they do exist, we can only rejoice at it, and there is no more to be said.

Angela was beginning to have an inkling of what had been the hidden purpose of her destiny. She had been led dead against what she had believed to be her own will, and she had followed the path on which she had been led, in spite of feeling uncertain and uneasy in doing so. Now she began to glimpse what was intended by her being as she was — a nun without the protection of the convent walls, without a home in which she could live under a spiritual mother, in community with spiritual sisters. The times called for new forms of regular life; what they were to be she did not yet know, but since her vision by the roadside at Brudazzo a profound and heart-felt calm had come over her. God would teach her what she was to do, when the time came.

For the present she continued to live as before — but the women who shared her thoughts and feelings and who gathered about Angela were increasing in number. They were daughters from farms and villages in the neighbourhood; Angela had known their families since she was a child. There was as yet no question of any organization; Angela and her friends went about performing such acts of charity as came to their hands. There was enough to do, God knows. Pestilence, war, bitter feuds between man and man, family and family — the final result was always the same: the sick dragged themselves along the highways till they could go no farther, men lay dying of their wounds in many homes, widows and mothers mourned their losses, and then there were all the children and the aged — .

The children, the little girls in particular, had always been the objects of Angela's most tender care. The first and most immediate task that had been conferred on her in the years of transition, when her mind was being finally moulded, was to be a mother to her little sister, when they were left orphans. Now she had abundance of little orphan sisters who needed her. And it came about quite naturally that, while nursing and clothing them and giving them food, she also taught them — the sacred story, the daily prayers, the catechism, the meaning of the Latin sentences that they heard in the Holy Mass. She asked those children whose fathers and mothers were alive to show their gratitude for this by being good and obedient; she trained her little girls in washing and cleaning, spinning and sewing, cooking and preparing medicines, bandaging wounds and nursing fever patients. And if any of them found amusement in turning over her books, Sister Angela was ready at once to teach them their letters.

Angela could read and write Italian and a little Latin. But she herself told several of her friends that she had never had any schooling. We know that her father and mother could read and write, and that her father was in the habit of reading aloud at home in the evenings, and that was Angela's greatest enjoyment. So it is likely enough that Angela learnt what she knew in the first place as a sort of child's game, and then she went on to teach herself — this is no more than many bright and intelligent children have done. Religious reading was now her only recreation, and her favourite books were those of the Fathers — to Angela Merici they were the friends of her childhood too. They now acquired a new meaning for her, when she read of their zeal for the education of little girls. Step by step she was approaching her goal.

She had made the acquaintance of a rich family from Brescia, the Patengolas, who had a country estate on Lake Garda, not far from Angela's home. The wife, Madonna Caterina, helped Angela in her charitable work with both money and personal assistance, but every year Angela had to go and stay a week with her at their country house. And the middle-aged spinster in her plain dark dress — the Franciscan Tertiaries wore no habit at that time, they were merely to dress as poor people — with her hair hidden by a simple white veil, mixed tactfully, cheerfully and at her ease with the convivial Renaissance men and women who formed the Patengolas' circle. Rides by the lake in the cool morning hours — Angela was a brilliant horsewoman — festive al fresco meals, music and song, talks about poetry and philosophy with people who were learned after the fashion of the Renaissance — because learning amused them — Angela took part in it all in her calm, direct, unobtrusive way, and she it was who was sought out by one after another of the gay company when they were in want of private sympathy or advice.

Brescia, " La Lionessa," had been called by Dante the proudest city in Lombardy. Milan and Venice had com-

peted to win her as an ally; within her walls faction
fights raged among the proud patrician families, outside
them she was assailed by army after army of foreign
troops or those of the Italian city-states. There was mortal enmity between two of the city's noble families,
which led to one of them, Avogadro, calling in Venice.
The other party, Gambaro, appealed to the French,
who had just undertaken an invasion of Northern Italy
Brescia was captured by the French under Bayard and
Gaston de Foix and suffered for a week a sack so cruel
as even to shock the people of that time — and they
were used to a good deal — accompanied by wholesale
executions of Avogadro's adherents. It was the ruin of
the French cause in Northern Italy, for the mercenaries
had won so rich a booty that they did not care to take
the field any more, and dispersed. The sack was followed by a pestilence, and then came poverty and distress which helped to spread infection over the country
districts, where beggars from the town were roaming.
Then the war blazed up again — and at last, in May
1516, the town capitulated after a long siege and made
peace with the French King. Angela heard of all the
misery from her friend, Donna Caterina. In the autumn,
after the Patengolas had returned to Brescia, they lost
both their little sons, and in her despair Caterina Patengola sent a message to Angela, asking her to come. Angela
started at once, and it was in these circumstances that
she made her way to Brescia — the place where it had
been announced to her in the vision that she was to
begin her work.

During that winter she stayed in Patengola's house, and considerately modified her ascetic habits as far as she could to avoid troubling her host and hostess. But one of the new friends she had found in their circle of acquaintance, the merchant Antonio Romano, saw how she would prefer to live. He offered her a couple of little rooms in a house he owned in one of the quietest parts of the town, and from the spring of 1517 for ten or twelve years she lived there, alone or with another solitary woman—"fasting, watching and praying," her biographers tell us. But all day long a stream of people passed in and out of Angela's bare little room. People of all classes and all stations, old and young, happy and sorrowful. Mothers seeking comfort in their troubles, young Renaissance beauties who were studying and writing poetry and had a fancy to talk to Angela about their spiritual life, prostitutes in search of help in their conversion or remedies for the diseases from which they suffered. Rich men came with well-filled purses, asking *la madre, la sorella* as the whole city now called her, to take them and do good with them, for no one could manage such things so kindly and thoughtfully as she. Young students came, often merely to have a look at the much talked-of *gentildonna*. One of these young blades came strutting in, resplendent with silk and redolent of perfume—he was studying theology, he told her, and he wished to ask the opinion of madre Angela, whether he had a call to the priesthood. "I can hardly believe it," replied Angela mildly; "for vanity is ill fitted for a priest. But come back another day, in another dress, and I will look at you more closely, and then we can talk about the matter." The fine gentleman came back, differently dressed — and he actually became a priest and died in the odour of sanctity. Another time it was two young noblemen who had kept the town on tenterhooks with their street fights and attempts to murder one another — it was arranged that they were to meet at Angela Merici's, so that she might try to reconcile them. The meeting began by the two mortal enemies drawing their swords and preparing to fall upon one another — Angela parted them, perfectly calm, and began to speak in a matter-of-fact tone, holding the two young men by the wrists; and when at last she got them to listen, her speech became pressing, ardent with love of their souls and zeal for the glory of God. They left her reconciled — and the story made such a sensation that Francesco Sforza himself made a detour to Brescia when he was in those parts, to inquire if it could be really true.

For that matter there was nothing in the mode of life Angela had chosen which might appear strange to her contemporaries: her having given away all her possessions and living on what people gave her; her serving all who needed her without reward; her subsisting for long periods from one Sunday to another without other food than the body of her Saviour in the Holy Communion; her watching and praying all through the night and only sleeping an hour or two towards morning on a sack of straw in a corner of the inner room — all these things they had seen many others do. Nor did anyone think it at all curious that she of all persons, who had lived all her life so purely and piously, should take the severest penance upon herself. The men and women of the Renaissance fought and loved and intrigued and enjoyed all that life could offer them in the way of intellectual pleasures and art and beauty and sensual gratification, but broadly speaking the old Catholic consciousness of the fundamental solidarity of mankind was still intact; they understood remarkably well why the pious madre Angela did penance in Brescia, and many of them certainly found comfort and edification in the thought that for her sake they might be given an opportunity of being reconciled to God before they died. She herself felt how intimately she was one with all these people; everything in them which found vent in violence and arrogance and defiance and lust existed potentially in her own soul — and she did penance because she was a human being, and the greater one's insight into God's perfection, the better one understands the meaning of man's defection.

Angela travelled much during these years. Ten or twelve hours in the saddle, half the night kneeling on the floor of a church — next morning in audience with the Duke of Milan who had sent for her, wishing her to assume the direction of all the poor relief in the city. A forced journey, on horseback as usual, to Castiglione to plead with the Prince on behalf of an outlaw. Posthaste to Cremona, where a pestilence had broken out and there was a shortage of nurses. And in 1524 she set out on a pilgrimage to Jerusalem, accompanied by her cousin Bartolomeo Biancosi and her friend Agostino

Romano. They sailed in a pilgrim ship from Venice, and then it came about that, while they were wind-bound off Crete, Angela was suddenly struck with blindness. In spite of that she continued her voyage. " Cannot you understand," she said to her companions, " that this blindness of mine may turn out for the good of my soul? " And her own opinion was that her having to pass in blindness, led by others, by all the places in Jerusalem where her Lord and Saviour had suffered and died, helped her to realize the passion of Christ in a deeper and more spiritual way than if she had been able to see and had been distracted by these new scenes and strange people. On the homeward voyage the ship which carried Angela met with terrible storms and was pursued by Algerine pirates. On their arriving at Crete Angela received her sight again, as suddenly as she had lost it. During her stay in Venice, where she lived in the hospital for incurables, she again received an offer from the city council to remain there and take charge of all public charitable institutions. But now she knew what it was she had to accomplish in the world, and she declined the Venetians' proposal.

While in Venice she had also seen Carpaccio's charming frescoes illustrating the legend of St. Ursula. Naturally the story of Ursula and the eleven thousand virgins was familiar to Angela, but possibly it was at this time that she first had the idea of placing her company under the protection of the virgin martyr.

During the jubilee year 1525 Angela visited Rome, and in an audience of the Pope, Clement VII, she no doubt confided to him her plan for establishing a company of virgins who were to devote themselves to the education of little girls and the preservation of home religious life. The Pope appears to have listened to her with sympathy, but to have had his doubts of the feasibility of such a plan. However, he expressed the opinion to his camerlengo that Angela was a woman of remarkable intellectual powers, and that it would have been a great gain to Rome if he had been able to persuade her to settle in the city and work there — but Donna Angela had declined with thanks all his proposals to that effect.

And when, a year or so later, a new Bishop was appointed to Brescia, Angela, in applying for his sanction and blessing, was already able to give him the names of the first twelve fellow-workers who had joined her. Our authorities describe them all as quite young, and they came from all classes of society — Barbara Fontana was Angela's foster-daughter, a poor orphan; Chiara Martinengo belonged to a princely family; the rest were daughters of small tradesmen, patricians, artisans and noblemen.

Angela had had recourse to primitive Christian forms which were known to her from reading the Fathers, since the maidens who had consecrated themselves to Christ continued to live each in her home and acted as apostles in those homes and as far outside them as they could reach; especially among children and young girls they were to promote by word and deed the same ideals as had sustained monastic life through the centuries.

I I I

But the multitude of women who could not be married or preferred not to marry, but had not the call nor the health nor the courage to enter a convent, was increasing year by year, as the constant wars thinned the ranks of young men and impoverished families, and as the ideas of the new age made headway and women too claimed the right to dispose of their own destinies. In reality the Renaissance entailed in many ways an emancipation of women from their old subjection to the family and its interests. What rendered possible the new type of Renaissance women, who intervened in politics, patronized art and scholarship, and themselves practised art and learning, was precisely this: that the Middle Ages had already recognized women's right to develop their talents freely, provided they really had a capacity for intellectual development. The former age had only acknowledged such talents when they were directed to religious life, since religion was the determining factor in the whole intellectual life of the Middle Ages; the new age acknowledged an intellectual life even when it was irreligious or anti-religious. But it was the Catholic Church which had provided the basis of this respect for an intellectual personality seeking self-expression and a field of activity, whether it were a man or a woman. We all know that where the culture of a country was moulded by Lutheranism or Calvinism, the women in the course of a few generations were brought up to be content with existing simply for the sake of the men. So that when the emancipation of women took place in such a country, it was to a great extent an accompani-

ment of the people's emancipation from their religious
traditions.

Angela had witnessed the first signs of the dissolu-
tion of the immemorial European idea of the family —
the solidarity of kinship to which both men and women
had sacrificed themselves and submitted, reluctantly or
willingly. And she had seen that in many places the religious life was in an advanced stage of decay — one
reason in point being that girls no longer submitted to
being sent to a nunnery simply because it suited their
parents to dispose of them in this way. It had seemed
natural enough for a mediæval father to determine that
this daughter or that was to be a nun — because he
could not find a suitable match for her, or because she
was not very pretty, or because his forefathers had given
property to a convent, thus establishing a tradition that
the convent in return received and provided for a
daughter of the family — it was often made a positive
condition, when a man bequeathed a piece of land to a
convent the income of which was sufficient to support
a nun, that his descendants should always have a prior
right to be provided for in this way. People of the Middle Ages saw nothing unreasonable in this; if the father
could betroth one daughter while still a child to the son
of a friend, in the assurance that he was acting for her
good, he must feel yet surer that the daughter whom he
betrothed to Christ would have the best Bridegroom of
all, if she did but contribute her good will — and from
the point of view of the family's eternal welfare it was
immensely reassuring to have a sister who could pray

for her kindred; they often had great need of pious intercession, as they all knew very well. But now there were startling tales of nuns absconding from convents where they had been placed involuntarily; renegade nuns made their appearance, demanding their share of the inheritance, demanding to be released from vows made under compulsion, demanding that the family should arrange a marriage for them, as for their sisters. Again, there were stories of men breaking into convents, carrying off nuns who would have been wealthy heiresses if they had not taken the veil; in many cases they tried to force the unhappy nun, in spite of her passionate protests, to declare that she had not chosen the religious life of her own free will. Even the walls of a convent afforded less and less security.

The prevailing corruption had assumed other sinister forms. In the years 1516 and 1524 Brescia and all the country round had been scared by rumours of witches' sabbaths which were said to have been celebrated at people's very doors — nay, in worthy people's houses, at night while good Christians were asleep. In Valcamonica alone two thousand women were alleged to be witches. The secular courts intervened and soon discovered that they were face to face with a sink of vice and blasphemy and perversity, a traffic in poison and black arts and heresy and crude superstition. So the matter was referred to the Inquisition. The last " enlightened " century has taught us to be scornful of superstition and indignant at the trials of witches — these were of course only old women who were a little more instructed and intelligent than their ignorant neighbours and the still more ignorant monks. Inquirers during the last twenty or thirty years have grasped rather more of the serious side of the matter: even those who for reasons of dogma do not believe in a personal devil have realized that in any case the witches did so, and that they did their best to establish a connection with the secret hosts of evil, the surest means of accomplishing which was to commit all the worst and most perverse acts that human imagination could devise. As with spiritualism in our own day so it was with mediæval witchcraft: around a kernel of supernatural phenomena were accumulated manifestations which were due to hysteria, fraud, the desire to make oneself interesting and to gain power over others, autosuggestion and sheer ignorance and superstition. That the cardinal remedy must be enlightenment, above all religious enlightenment, was clear enough to the majority — but the problem of spreading enlightenment so widely as to do any good appeared hopeless to most of those who thought over the matter, in the confused and unhappy state in which things were.

And then the new heresies from the countries north of the Alps penetrated to Lombardy. The embers of earlier heresies, those of the Albigenses, were still smouldering here and there, and now all these new doctrines swept down like a blast and fanned them into flame. Baptism, the holy sacrifice of the Mass, confession, the authority of the Church were attacked — as always — by reformers and atheists simultaneously. The sanctity of marriage was denied on both sides, chastity was scoffed at as an impossibility and a sin against nature.

It is altogether difficult for us, in our time, to form an idea of *how* bold Angela's plan was. The life of the convent needed renewing — Angela knew this and knew that *she* was not to bring it about. A reformation was needed within the Church — Angela did not yield to the temptation of taking a hand in this, although she saw clearly enough that the priesthood was not all it might be. " Be on your guard," she writes to her spiritual daughters, " lest any confessor or monk weaken your right feeling towards fasting or virginity or other good things, for there are many of these who under pretext of giving good advice confuse the minds of poor maidens and cause them to abandon their good resolutions in spite of their own better knowledge." And she lays down in her Rule that none of her daughters may take a new confessor without the consent of her superiors in the Company. " In these dangerous times your only support will be in taking refuge at the feet of Jesus Christ; He will direct and teach you." And elsewhere she writes to her Company: " Know that you have to defend and protect your little lambs against wolves and against thieves — two kinds of dangerous folk, to wit, false and worldly friars with their errors, and heretics."

Angela Merici was clear as to her own task: *she* was to work for the renewal of religious life at home, among the children, and in the first place she was to influence the girls who in due time would build up new homes and be the mothers of the next generation. And above all her Company was to try to come in contact with that section of the people who were unable or disinclined to attend to their children's schooling, especially that of their little daughters.

And to undertake this work Angela had founded her Company of virgins, under the banner of St. Ursula — the brave British princess who according to the legend assembled an army of eleven thousand virgins and set out on a pilgrimage in ships which were steered and rowed by the virgins themselves, and who with her flock saved Cologne by their martyrdom outside the city, since the Huns were so terrified by the miracles that took place over the bodies of the murdered virgins that they raised the siege and fled. For Angela knew that the life of her daughters would be one of continued conflict in dead earnest: they were to go on living in their homes and assuredly this would not always be so easy for them; it was conceivable that many fathers and mothers would be by no means delighted to have their daughter about the house and to witness her endeavours to lead a perfect Christian life, to have her running off to Mass every morning before they were up. And even if she did all in her power to make herself useful and no charge on her home, there would certainly be some who let her know that she was a burden on her family in following her passion for tending poor children and keeping school for them. There might also be a danger of infection: it must be remembered that the hospitals, which were all charitable institutions, often had foundlings' homes attached to them, and we know that it was especially the children in the hospitals that the Ursulines in the beginning took charge of and educated.

Some years doubtless passed from the time Angela had gathered about her the first little band of girls before she gave a definite form and a Rule to St. Ursula's Company. For her confessor relates how she confided to him that she had had a vision: one night while at prayer she saw an angel standing before her with a whip in his hand, and with an expression of anger in his countenance and attitude he struck her with the whip, saying God had sent him to chastise her for being so dilatory and timid a servant. And when she was overwhelmed with sorrow and began to beg forgiveness for her weakness, Jesus Christ Himself appeared to her and reproached her with her want of faith.

In the spring of 1537, then, Angela called together her Company to its first chapter, in order that the sisters might elect a Mother General and four Mother Assistants according to the Rule which Angela had prepared and communicated to the Ursulines in advance. The Company at this time numbered seventy-two members. In addition to these, four widows belonging to the leading families of Brescia had associated themselves with the work. The meeting was held in an oratory in the house of one of these ladies, Elisabetta Prato, and for the time being the sisters met there for a solemn Mass followed by a chapter of the Order on the last Sunday of the month, and for Mass and communion on the first Friday of the month. Apart from this the Rule obliged the Ursulines to hear Mass at least once daily in their own parish church, accompanied, if possible, by their family. The original Rule does not prescribe any habit in the strict sense — merely that the sisters are to dress simply and modestly and to wear an opaque white veil as a sign that they have dedicated themselves to the service of God.

At the head of the whole Company is the Mother General, who is elected for life, supported by a council of four Assistants. In every town where companies of St. Ursula's virgins are established, *donne governante* are to be elected, one for each section of the town; Brescia was divided into eight sections with eight *donne governante* — lady governors. These are to have charge of all the members in their respective sections. They have under them teachers, whose duty it is to teach the girls what is enjoined by the Rule, but it is incumbent on the lady governors to be acquainted with the girls' circumstances and ready to help any who need it; while their first care must be for their souls, it is also an act of charity to assist them materially, especially when any member of the Company falls into ill health or poverty. If a sister loses her home owing to a death or other misfortune, the lady governor is to find her a suitable place of abode either in another family or together with one or more sisters who are in the same position. When a sister is so ill that her life is in danger, the lady governor must go to her accompanied by two sisters and nurse her and see that she has all the support which the Church

I I 9

offers to her dying. If she dies, it is again the lady governor who is responsible for giving the sister burial and reporting the death to the Mother General and to the Company's spiritual Father, in order that Masses may be said for the dead and her sisters may remember her in their prayers. " But above all," says the Rule, " she must love the sisters who are under her protection with such profound and true affection as she owes to the promised brides and dear children of Jesus Christ, must cherish them with motherly tenderness, not regarding them as lowly, insignificant women, but in their person loving God, for the love of whom they have taken upon themselves this task."

The teachers are to instruct the sisters in the Rule, its wording and spirit. And under them is the band of girls who are to endeavour to practise Christian perfection, each in her own home. That is: in the first place to keep the commandments of God and the commandments of the Church, openly to pay the Majesty of God that veneration which is the duty of all mankind, but which they have specially bound themselves to fulfil. Peculiar stress is laid on the fourth commandment: above all in their homes the sisters are to strive to imitate Our Lord and His Mother by showing themselves full of affection, patience, meekness and goodness. But as far as they can they are also required to perform acts of charity outside their homes, each according to her capacity and subject to the advice of her confessor; and above all they are to instruct children, especially little girls from poor homes which cannot afford their schooling and from ignorant surroundings, in the doctrines of Christian faith and morals.

" Let them stand fast in their holy resolution or by their vow (those of the sisters who have made such a vow) to preserve their virginity, not only their bodily virginity which, if once lost, can never be regained, but also that of the spirit, laying it to heart that in order to attain this they must keep watch on their five senses." " They are not obliged on peril of sin to keep those fasts which are counselled by the Rule, but we beg them to try to put these counsels in practice, so far as their health permits and they are advised by their confessor." If it is possible for them to attend Mass every morning, they are to do so, and also to pray for a while after Mass, saying a part of the office or their rosary in church. But they must not stay in church longer than is necessary for their prayers (at that time the churches were still places where one met everybody, where there was constantly something going on, weddings, christenings, Masses for corporations and guilds, and they were the rendezvous of people who wanted to hear or retail gossip). If they are late in returning, it may cause trouble at home; and by their work in the home they acquire great inner sanctity and set an example by their unselfish life.

In this way Angela had created a system whereby her Company in its work could penetrate to the core of the families — a new instrument, at the same time powerful and elastic, for a religious renaissance; and unmarried women and widows were to be the workers.

Under the Mother General, who has a priest, chosen by the sisters, as her adviser, is the council of assistants, and at the head of each local branch are governing and teaching mothers who are acquainted with local conditions, below them are the sisters who are billeted so to speak among private homes, the novices and the girls of from twelve to eighteen who are received into the Company in order to become acquainted with its life, but are not allowed to bind themselves before they are grown up; and around each individual Ursuline are grouped those children who have been confided to her by their parents for education.

Angela lays it down very decidedly that in her Company class distinctions are to be *ignored;* the young lady of the nobility who can teach her pupils to read and her maid who can teach them to spin and sew and scour are equally welcome in St. Ursula's society, and since they both teach the children Christianity in theory and practice they are sisters within the Company.

The Rule provides for meetings — general chapters, chapters for all Ursulines in one and the same town, sectional meetings for sisters in the same district, and meetings in Brescia attended by representatives from other towns to which the Company had penetrated. For Angela was certain that her work had a future before it and would spread far and wide from Brescia.

Angela herself was elected as General of the Company at the first chapter — much against her will. She was now a woman of over sixty; from her young days she had led the most Spartan of lives in ceaseless self-sacrifice, hard work for others, continual effort in the cause of humanity, always at the service of those who besieged her two little rooms. Add to this fasting and nights wholly spent in prayer and in ecstasies — of which she herself says little, but her foster-daughter, Barbara Fontana, related what she had seen, after the saint's death. She herself would have been glad to retire, now that her work was set in motion — to withdraw to some form of solitude. But she bowed to the decision of her daughters and was the Ursulines' " dolce Madre Suor Angela " for the years that remained to her.

A great deal of what she wrote for the guidance of her daughters — and for those who were to direct the Company after her — is still in existence. It is apparent on every page that consciously and unconsciously Angela saw it as her call to bring about a radical reform in the direction of the ancient Christian ideals: it is as virgin and as mother that women can and must be a power in the community, showing themselves worthy of the salvation so dearly bought for them by the Son of God, and deserving of the honour and glory He has promised to all His own. St. Ursula's Company was enlisted against the new paganism of the Renaissance and against the Reformers' degradation of women, and Mother Angela's counsels and last will were written to render it efficient.

The increased interest of the Renaissance in each human being as an individual is shared by Angela — but in her case it applies to each individual soul. " I beseech you, bear each one of your sisters individually in your hearts, not merely their names, but the conditions in which they live at the time, their character and disposition, in short, their whole lives." But at the same time she begs them: "Love all your daughters with equal affection, so that you have no more pronounced fondness for one than for the rest." For " I address to you as a prayer my last words, which I repeat, and I would gladly write them with my blood — preserve unity and harmony, so that you have but one heart and one will."

She reminds the superiors that to a mother each child is as dear as if it were the only one, and bids them be mindful of the joy it gives a mother to be able to dress her children handsomely and make them attractive. Should not a mother in St. Ursula's Company be equally eager to dress every one of her children so that it may win grace in the eyes of God? And " reflect that in reality you have a greater need to serve them than they have of your service. . . . Be ever watchful to find out what they need, spiritually and temporally; if you yourselves have not the wherewithal to help them, then go to your superiors. Take from yourselves, but do not let them lack anything." " Do not lose heart, even if you should discover that you lack qualities necessary for the work to which you are called. He who called you will not desert you, but the moment you are in need He will stretch out His saving hand." But " how can you correct them if it is a case of a fault which they can see in yourselves? " " I entreat of you meekly that you try to win all with affection and with a gentle hand and

with sweetness, not with harsh commands. Look at
Jesus Christ, who says: ' Learn of me, because I am
meek, and humble of heart.' Do not teach them to be
hard and discourteous in their speech, but friendly, with
a mind full of goodwill and Christian charity." For the
maiden who has given her troth to Christ ought to feel
that her heart is filled with joy, love, faith and hope in
God. " Live always on your living hope. How many
are there among the rich, queens, noble ladies, who are
unable to find peace amidst their superabundance and
splendour, by reason of their extreme poverty of spirit,
while the poor who give alms live abundantly in consolation and courage." " Keep together in the bond of
affection, sharing all things with each other and supporting each other in Jesus Christ."

These counsels are taken for the most part from the
testament which Angela Merici made her secretary,
Gabriele Gozzano, read out to the members of the
Company whom she had summoned to her death-bed.
She fell sick in the spring of 1539; a lingering fever, such
as is well known in the climate of Italy, was slowly sap-
ping the old Mother's vitality. For months together she
was almost confined to her bed, but from it she continued to direct her Company, to train those sisters
whom she wished to be elected as Mother General and
Assistants after her decease, and in addition to receive
the innumerable visitors who wished to speak with her
or merely to have a sight of the celebrated Angela
Merici. And one day, just after New Year 1540, when
she knew herself that the end was very near, she sum-

moned her sisters to her and had her testament read out to them.

" Beware of trying to accomplish anything by force, for God has given every single person free will and desires to constrain none; He merely shows them the way, invites them and counsels them; as in the words of St. John: ' I counsel you to buy an incorruptible crown.' ' I counsel thee,' He says, not ' I force thee.'

" I shall continue to be more alive than I was in this life, and I shall see you better and shall love yet more the good deeds which I shall see you doing continually, and I shall be able to help you more." These were her last words to St. Ursula's Company.

The Sunday before she died a young relative of hers had come from Salò to hear High Mass in the cathedral of Brescia. During the sermon the priest asked the prayers of the congregation for Suor Angela who lay at the point of death. The young man rushed to his great-aunt's house and found Angela up; she stood washing her hair. She chatted cheerfully with the lad, and he went away comforted, feeling sure that she could not be in such a bad way. But she had sent her nurses to church, wishing to wash and attire herself without assistance, so as to save the trouble of those who were to lay out her body. She then asked to be given the sacraments of the dying, once more took leave of her daughters and gave them a dying mother's blessing. After that she caused herself to be dressed in the habit of a Franciscan nun and bade the nurses lay her on the floor upon the mat on which she had been used to sleep while in health, with a wooden billet as pillow. From that moment she seemed to be caught up in a sort of ecstasy, her great eyes gazed upward, as though looking already into the other world, now and again those who stood by heard her whisper " Jesus, Jesus," and the little old face seemed to shine with its own light. All at once it was as though Mother Angela awoke from her trance — she looked about her with a last loving smile for her nurses and for her confessor who was praying for the departing soul, and then she said in her accustomed clear and gentle voice: " In manus tuas, Domine, commendo spiritum meum." Then she expired.

This was in the evening of January 27, 1540, and the same night it was all over the city that la santa was no more. Early next morning her friends had to lay her on the bier and place her in St. Afra's church on the other side of the road, and then the procession of people who wished to see her for the last time filed incessantly through the church — for thirty days she lay unburied, with her face uncovered. Meanwhile the canons of the cathedral, who pointed out that the Ursulines' oratory was situated in their parish; the Franciscans, who argued that she was a Tertiary of their Order, and the priests of St. Afra's, who could claim that she belonged to their congregation — were disputing as to where Angela Merici's body should be interred. It was a somewhat unedifying comedy which unfortunately was performed very often in the Middle Ages, when anyone died in the odour of sanctity. The end of it was that Angela's relatives were able to produce a licence she had obtained from Rome, which gave her permission to be buried in St. Afra's church, since the first martyr Bishop of Brescia and his companions in martyrdom lay there.

Meanwhile the crowds poured in and out to see the marvel — Angela's body underwent no change, no sign of corruption appeared, but a faint scent as of white roses was exhaled by it and filled the church. And for the first time painters and sculptors had an opportunity of portraying the old Suor Angela who had never consented to sit to anyone while alive. Then she was buried at the city's expense — and Angela Merici, who had given away all she possessed more than thirty years before and had since lived on what her fellow-Christians were willing to give her or such part of it as she did not give away again to those in need — was accorded, her biographers tell us, a princely funeral.

4

AND people continued to ask help of the dead Angela Merici, as they had asked it of her when alive. Her native town, Dezensano, was the first to acknowledge her cult publicly, when the town council appointed her its protectress and *advocata,* and erected a memorial chapel on the Mericis' old farm outside the town.

Although Urban VIII decreed in 1631 that public worship was to be offered to none but canonized saints, Angela was given the honours of a saint wherever her

Order penetrated, and the Holy See recognized January 27 as her festival — it was altered later to May 31. The French Ursulines were the first to have a special office for her, and all over the Catholic world altars were dedicated and statues set up of Beata Angela Merici. The solemn canonization did not take place until 1807, after which a statue of her, clad in the habit of the French Ursulines, was placed in St. Peter's among the statues of the other founders of Orders.

But by that time St. Angela Merici's Company of St. Ursula had already undergone many changes, and Angela's nuns without a convent who were to penetrate society in its separate cells, the families, had become the conventual Order of the Ursulines. Angela had not obtained the approbation of Rome for her work at the time of her death, and scarcely was she gone when a host of objections appeared — mostly from parents, especially rich parents, who preferred to see their daughters either married or in a nunnery, so that they should not be left alone in the world when their natural protectors were no more. Friends of Angela, above all the priest Dom Tribesco, championed her idea: " Enter the first church you come to, go where you will about the streets, and you will meet her daughters. It is a joy and a marvel," wrote the eloquent Italian, " to see these heavenly doves collect about the fountain of the Lord to wash their wings of the smallest speck, nourish themselves with the corn of the elect, quench their thirst in the wine of virginity, and return to their homes with soul and heart fixed upon heavenly things. Formerly such blessings could only be enjoyed within the convent walls, but in our day they are to be had in the world, and this is due to the work of Angela Merici." And he points out that among the Ursulines there are many whose first duty is plainly towards old and infirm parents and mothers too poor to hire help, or who are otherwise called to perform God's work in ways that are impossible to cloistered nuns.

St. Ursula's Company spread over the whole of Northern Italy, while disputes as to the final form it was to take were still raging furiously. In 1566 St. Charles Borromeo wrote to the Company's spiritual Father in Brescia asking for information, and received this answer: " The Company has given Sisters to all the hospitals of Brescia. It maintains schools for girls and gives them Christian instruction. God has used it as His instrument for the conversion of souls and for winning to His service many families where one of these Sisters has her home. . . . It is indeed a marvel of God's power and goodness to see these frail young girls in whom the spirit of Agnes and Agatha is reborn and who dwell unharmed in the midst of dangers and scandals." St. Charles Borromeo induced the Ursulines to establish a Company in Milan, which he supported in every way, and in return it was the Ursulines who were foremost in helping him during the two terrible plague years in Milan. He also instituted a college for girls and placed their education entirely in the hands of the Ursulines. At the same time he presented them with a building in which they could live together, instead of being scattered about the town, and obtained the Pope's confirmation of the Company's right to own and inhabit this house collectively " senza esser di clausura."

That is to say that, whereas formerly nuns had made a solemn vow which bound them to live within the convent walls and never to go outside them — without express dispensation on account of extraordinary circumstances — or outside those buildings which are closed to all but the inmates of the convent, being as a rule only allowed to speak with their own relatives through a grating — this house of the Ursulines in Milan was doubtless the first of those homes for Sisters of an Order, those congregations of women, which after the Reformation contributed so enormously to the life of the Church. All the congregations which arose later — hospital Sisters, Sisters who nurse patients in their homes, those who undertake visiting, teaching and missionary work — are in a way descendants of St. Angela Merici's family.

The result, as far as her own daughters were concerned, was that the forces which strove to make of the Ursulines a cloistered Order won the day. Even as a cloistered Order of nuns St. Angela's daughters have succeeded in preserving many of their Mother's features. Her educational principles regarding religious instruction and the individual treatment of each child have remained characteristic of the Ursulines; in addition to the customary convent vows they solemnly promise to devote themselves entirely to the education of girls on a solid basis of religious instruction. They have accompanied the missionaries among Indians and Negroes and

Asiatics, they have made important contributions to the study of the psychology of coloured races, written works on Indian languages and African dialects, they were among the first Orders of nuns to allow their Sisters to take university examinations and doctors' degrees. Their convents have been burnt by redskins and stoned by mobs of whites — and St. Angela's daughters have not given in, but have calmly set to work to build them up again. The Ursulines have gone to the guillotine, singing their office and encouraging their companions on the way to the scaffold. — Continued attempts have also been made, especially in France, to re-establish St. Ursula's Company according to the primitive Rule, and from time to time small companies of Ursulines have existed, scattered among their homes, especially in the smaller towns of southern and central France.

And the new direction which St. Angela gave to the system of religious Orders has been followed by others. Mary Ward tried to establish a sisterhood of nuns without a convent: they were to go out as governesses to the English Catholic families who were fighting to preserve the faith of their fathers through persecution and suppression at home or in exile on the Continent. Mary Ward, who was born in 1589, struggled in vain for her idea — her institute she called it; and it took a form other than that she had planned, when at last " Les dames anglais," " Die englischen Fräuleins," " The Ladies of Loretto " as they call themselves in America, spread over the Catholic world with their educational institutions and high schools for girls.

St. Jeanne de Chantal had also intended that the Visitants, the Order that she founded, should go out nursing the sick, visiting the poor and instructing the ignorant. St. Francis de Sales defended St. Chantal's ideas,
and he pointed to the fact that something similar had
been practised in Italy, with excellent results, produc-
ing a copy of St. Angela's primitive Rule. But this time
again it ended in the Visitants being made into a conventual Order; and under the modified forms which
this necessitated they were then allowed to take up the
work to which they had been called; namely receiving
sick, aged or otherwise infirm women and giving them
an opportunity of leading a life of prayer and seclusion
under a mild Rule.

St. Vincent de Paul took up once more the banner of
St. Angela, and it was reserved for him, with his " Filles
de Charité," finally to realize the idea of a monastic life
for women without a convent. He was a contemporary
of Mother Mary Ward and a personal friend of St. Francis de Sales, and he had worked for years in Marseilles
and Toulouse, where the Ursulines had large schools for
poor girls. He had been confessor to the nuns of the
Visitation. The wars of religion had wrought further
havoc in Europe, neo-paganism continued to disinte-
grate the old forms of society, corruption and distress
had assumed sinister proportions in the growing great
towns — the need of Sisters who could go out and serve
the poor and sick in their homes was simply crying.
Nevertheless it took St. Vincent de Paul twenty years to
overcome the resistance of King and parliament and the

cautious apprehensions of Popes and cardinals. And at last he laid down the line to be followed by the new type of religious Sisters. He writes: " The convent of the Sister of Charity is to be the home of the sick, her cell the sick-room, her chapel the parish church, her cloister the streets of the town or the corridors of the hospital. Obedience is to be her seclusion, the fear of God her grating and modesty her veil."

After the tempest of the Renaissance and the Reformation was passed, the old Orders mustered their veterans, many of them were reformed from within and radically, some sooner than others. It was seen that they possessed vitality and had a right to survive. But there was need in addition of the new and freer forms. And there are still germs in the ideas of St. Angela Merici which have not reached development; it may yet be that la grande madre suor Angela will give life to new families within the great home of the Church, and new generations will arise and call her blessed.

ROBERT SOUTHWELL, S.J.

PRIEST, POET, MARTYR

IT was in one of the new Catholic churches in England — I do not remember which, but I believe it was one of the churches in Newcastle. I had entered it one day, when I was over there in 1928. The walls of this church were covered to a certain height with white tiles, each of which bore the name of an English saint, from the early days of Roman missionaries and Anglo-Saxon martyrs and Fathers down to the martyrs of Tudor and Stuart times. The two first names that I happened to see, from the bench where I was kneeling, were those of Ven. Edmund Arrowsmith and Ven. Robert Southwell. — I will not pretend that the idea was very attractively carried out — glazed white tiles with green lettering have, to say the least of it, an unusual effect in the decoration of a church. But the intention was clear enough — to express the way in which all churches have been built up. Before the cathedrals there were the catacombs; since then objects of value have been piled about our altars, but beneath every altar slab there must be a " tomb " — a shrine with the relics of a martyr — and upon the tomb the chalice with the precious Blood of Christ must stand. All the impressive splendour with which the Mass has gradually been surrounded ought in any case to remind *us* of Masses which were celebrated in haste and secrecy, while death lay in wait beside the very altar, and priest and congregation knew, whenever they received the sacraments, that this might be the viaticum.

 WHEN Henry VIII broke with Rome, it was not his intention to make a Protestant country of England. It is incorrect to speak of Henry VIII's "divorce" — Henry was sufficiently versed in theology not to imagine that marriages can be dissolved. As quite a young man he had been married to his brother's widow, Catherine of Aragon, and when dispensation was granted for this marriage nobody believed that Catherine and the sickly, half-grown Prince Arthur had ever lived together as husband and wife. (The father of Arthur and Henry, Henry VII, had himself thought of marrying his dead son's bride, in order to retain her dowry and the family connection. However, he saw in time that after all this was more than his people would stand!)

The eldest son of Henry VIII and Catherine died when a few months old, and afterwards the Queen bore one dead or death-doomed child after another — her daughter Mary alone grew up. When it became clear to everyone that Queen Catherine would never give

England a prince, the idea occurred to the King that he must be able to find a pretext for putting away his wife and marrying a French princess. Cardinal Wolsey favoured the plan. He was one of those Renaissance princes of the Church who brought disgrace and injury upon her, but he served the new political ideas of the age with great strength of will and with an industry that is quite prodigious — unfortunately there was a sad want of proportion between his will and his capacity as a politician. The failure of the Cardinal's dynastic policy was due, however, to the King's infatuation for Anne Boleyn, who would not yield to Henry for any less price than the title of Queen.

But when, about 1524, Henry decided to put away his Queen, he availed himself of the pretext of scruples of conscience: the dispensation for his marriage with his brother's widow had been granted on false assumptions, for Catherine had been Prince Arthur's wife not merely in name.

It was one of the many harmful practices that had become fairly common towards the close of the Middle Ages that wealthy and influential people who wished to be released from their marriage and to contract a fresh connection under an appearance of legitimacy applied to the ecclesiastical authorities alleging that they had been united in spite of the existence of obstacles — blood relationship, or spiritual relationship for which one had neglected to obtain dispensation, compulsion of the woman to live in matrimony without having given her consent, or the like. Then if the other party to the marriage did not enter a protest — if, that is, husband and wife for one reason or another had agreed to part — the marriage was *not dissolved,* but declared *invalid.* The relation had never been one of lawful marriage, the parties in reality were still unmarried, and so no one could forbid them to marry now.

But Catherine the Spaniard was a woman jealous of her honour and deeply religious; neither promises nor threats nor political considerations were able to move her. She refused to admit that she had lived in incest with King Henry, that her dead children and her young daughter were born out of wedlock. She defended her honour to the utmost, and thus Rome was unable to provide Henry with the declaration he required — that his marriage was invalid and that he was a bachelor and free to take a wife.

The result was that Henry broke with Rome, declared himself Supreme Head of the Church in England, got Parliament — which he held in his hand — to assert that it was high treason to deny the King's right to this title. For the future he arranged his marriages as suited himself — a bloody tragi-comedy it was — drove the monks and nuns out of their convents and appropriated to himself all property that had belonged to the Orders, plundered the churches of their possessions, including the innumerable foundations, great and small, the incomes of which were designed to maintain schools for the people. Even in Henry VIII's time Thomas More could write, with reference to the Reformers' pretension that everyone should form his own opinion of religion by independent reading of the Bible, that scarcely half the population of England, men, women and children, were able to read at all. A hundred years later it was computed that nine-tenths of the people were illiterate, and of the one-tenth that had some schooling the greater part had received it through the small remnant of institutions that still survived from mediæval times. Henry VIII was on the point of dealing with the Universities when death put a stop to his activities.

It was because they refused to acknowledge that a king can be the Supreme Head of the Church in his country that Bl. Cardinal Fisher, Bl. Thomas More, the Bridgetine Richard Reynolds, the Carthusian Fathers from London's Charterhouse and the long procession of abbots and monks of the different Orders were condemned as traitors and executed under Henry VIII.

Now it was the fact that in the sixteenth and seventeenth centuries (and long after) there were not many people in the whole of Europe who believed that a State could practise religious tolerance and still endure. The basis of this view was the acknowledgment of the truth: that a nation's life and destiny are determined first and foremost by its religion.

In those countries where the Catholics had control, they did their best to extirpate Protestantism — which even then had split up into a vast number of sects, some of which have died out long ago, while others have given rise to those we now know. In those countries where one or another of the new religious forms had found favour with those in power, the adherents of the old religion were persecuted. On both sides the struggle was carried on with cruelty, and the cruelty was sustained with a ferocious logic which terrifies us of the present day. — Though the Great War has shown us how cruel methods of fighting can be carried out with inflexible consistency by the men who are responsible for their people's fate and believe that a nation's life is dependent on the result of the struggle. — If Calvinists and Catholics were able for long periods to live side by side in France, if not peaceably, at any rate in mutual toleration, working together in the civil service and in the army, then both parties made a virtue of necessity; circumstances had involved it. The mass of the people were Catholics, but the mass of the wealthy classes were Calvinists.

To a modern historian who tries to be just it may appear that there was no great difference: in England the King — or Queen — hanged and quartered Catholics for not sharing his religion. In France and Spain the King burned Protestants for the same reason. Torture, banishment, confiscation of fortune, were the means employed everywhere. May we not say that there was nothing to choose between them?

In the sixteenth century people thought there was a difference. In Spain and in France the Protestants were trying to destroy the ancient traditions of the people, to overthrow the order upon which the life of the nation as well as their own lives were founded. And they saw that in England and Scotland the Catholics claimed a right for the faith which had not only shown itself compatible with the order of society, but had been the main factor in the creation of that order and in the birth of the nation. This was the answer given by Bl. John Ogilvie, when he appeared before the court in Edinburgh, in December 1613: " Neither Francis has forbidden France, nor does Philip burn for religion but for heresy, which is not religion but rebellion."

And the heir of Drum-na-Keith, who had forsaken his family, his home and his estate to become a Jesuit and a priest, says to Spottiswoode and the other reformed clergymen who owed their position and all they possessed to the favour of King James:

" The King cannot forbid me my own country, since I am just as much a natural subject as the King himself. . . . What more do we owe to him than our ancestors to his ancestors? If he has all his right to reign from his ancestors, why does he ask for more than they have left him by right of inheritance? They have never had any spiritual jurisdiction, nor have they ever exercised any; nor held any other faith than the Roman Catholic."

But what had made this Scottish laird's son return to the faith of his fathers and forego his heritage in this world, was the result of a passionate course of theological studies and ardent prayers for light. The baronet of Drum-na-Keith had sent his eldest son abroad with the intention that young Johnnie should study for a few years on the continent. But this too is characteristic of the violent religious turmoil of the age: the boy of fifteen was entirely absorbed by an interest in religion — and what he wanted to be clear about was this: which faith is the *true* one? He himself explained later that

what decided the question for him was his experience
that the Catholic Church included all kinds of people —
emperors and kings, princes and noblemen, as well as
burghers, peasants and beggars — but that it overtopped
them all, no man was above the Church. And he had
seen that it could impel men and women of all classes to
renounce the whole world, to abandon all they possessed
in order to devote themselves entirely to a life in God,
for God. And the final reason, the one which in the end
led to his conversion, was his having seen that the men
who gave their lives and their blood for Christ, those
who had died to spread Christianity among mankind,
had been martyrs for the Christianity of Rome and not
for that of Geneva or Wittenberg. At the age of seventeen John Ogilvie returned to Catholicism, because he
wished to belong to the Church of the martyrs. Twenty
years later he himself suffered the death of a martyr.

2

HENRY VIII's son by Jane Seymour, Edward VI, was
marked from birth — like all Henry VIII's children — by
the new and sinister disease which in reality is of such immense historical significance, precisely because it contributed to determine the mentality of the Renaissance and
the Reformation: the megalomaniacal, self-worshipping,
unrestrained, egocentric tendency in the men of that time
was often wholly or in part a consequence of their having
syphilis. The malady devastated Europe to an extent

which the historians of last century have insisted on ig-
noring: for one thing it would have been highly improper
in the nineteenth century to have any such knowledge,
and in addition it was an article of faith that the Reformation and the Renaissance definitely meant progress —
and the historians of the Victorian age and their Conti-
nental contemporaries could not very well acknowledge
the pale spirochæte as a factor in the march of progress.
Not only the liberation from old moral " prejudices," but
the prevailing habits of eating and drinking — everyone
helped himself from the dish with fingers or spoon —
the conditions of social life and travelling — in country
houses and inns strangers were packed together in the
same bed, as many as it would hold — the crowding in
towns, and the replacing of defective mediæval cleanli-
ness by the shocking filthiness of the Renaissance —
everything prepared the way for the triumphant progress of the spirochæte through Europe.

Edward VI was born sick and succumbed to his dis-
order before he was grown up. The unhappy boy was
treated with preparations of mercury so strong as to
ruin the hands of the maids who washed his linen (the
tragedy of the Tudors has been dealt with from a medi-
cal point of view in Dr. C. MacLaurin's book *De Mor-
tuis*). The real rulers of England in his time were his
mother's relatives. They had grown immensely rich on
the estates of churches and convents and were zealous
" Anti-Papists."

He was succeeded by his half-sister Mary Tudor, the
daughter of Henry and Catherine. She has been called

"the bloody." Her attempt to bring England back to the Catholic Church was a failure, though not because the fires of Smithfield made her specially unpopular at the time. She owed her unpopularity to her Spanish marriage, to her predilection for everything Spanish, but above all to the fear of those of the nobility who had been enriched by the estates of church and convent that they might be forced to restore some of this wealth. That part of it which was under the Crown was loyally made good by the Queen, but it was comparatively little: the fantastic sums which had passed into Henry VIII's hands had run through his fingers like sand.

Elizabeth again broke with Rome, and once more priests and laymen were condemned to death for refusing to acknowledge the Queen as Supreme Head of the Church. So that when the Queen's bishop, my lord of Winchester, in a theological discussion with his prisoner, Mr. Robert Anderton — a newly ordained priest from Rheims who looked so young that people took him for no more than a child — began talking about the old legendary figure Pope Joan, Mr. Anderton replied with a flippant remark about Pope Elizabeth.

Prior to 1585 the charge of treason was based on various grounds. Bl. Edmund Campion and the whole band of priests who were executed with him were accused of having formed a conspiracy against the Queen's life. Most of these priests had never seen one another until they met in court. But false witnesses, who were a special feature of the time, came forward as usual. The priests Hanse, Lacy, Kirkman and others were condemned to death for having " seduced the Queen's subjects to disobedience " — they had heard confessions and given absolution. The Act of 1585 made it high treason to have been ordained priest by a Catholic Bishop, and simple treason to have housed or abetted a priest.

The penalty for a layman under this Act of Parliament was death by hanging. The penalty for high treason in England was hanging, but the victim was cut down while still alive, castrated, disembowelled, his heart was torn out and burnt together with the entrails. The body was quartered and the pieces were dipped in boiling pitch to preserve them; after that the head and quarters were set up on poles in suitable positions near the place of execution, as a warning to sympathizers.

The penalty for having had other dealings with the outlawed priests was liable to vary according to local feeling and the sentiments of the judges — cases occurred of people getting off fairly lightly after such indiscretions. But on the other hand a man might be hanged for having stood a priest a tankard of ale. Mr. Thomas Bosgrave had taken off his hat and crammed it on the head of Mr. Cornelius, when the Jesuit was being carried away as a prisoner — " The honour I owe to your function may not suffer me to see you go bareheaded." Mr. Bosgrave was instantly arrested, led away and hanged together with Mr. Cornelius.[1]

1 At that time priests in England were addressed and referred to as Mr. So-and-So. It was not till about the middle of the nineteenth century that it became customary to call all Catholic priests " Father," following the practice of Irish Catholics.

3

ROBERT SOUTHWELL's ancestors for many generations had occupied manors great and small in Suffolk and Norfolk and had intermarried with the best families of those counties. It sometimes happened that a man of their line entered the King's service and received fiefs from him. But the majority had stayed at home on their lands, living as country gentlemen, managing their farms, hunting, fighting, bargaining and feasting.

One of Holbein's most famous portraits — in the Uffizi — immortalizes Sir Richard Southwell's picturesque features. Sir Richard had been a courtier of Henry VIII, had taken an active part in the suppression of the monasteries and had received as his share of the booty, amongst other things, an ancient Benedictine priory, Horsham St. Faith. Under Edward and later under Mary he changed his political and religious convictions a few times and appears to have made a profit on it every time. His private life was somewhat irregular — while his first wife was still alive he had two sons by a poor relative of hers, a girl of the Darcy family of Danbury. He afterwards married her and made good provision for his two sons. But the bulk of his property went to legitimate collateral heirs. (In England bastards were not legitimatized by the subsequent marriage of their parents.)

His elder son with the bar sinister was also named Richard. He married the daughter of a neighbouring gentleman, of the family from which Percy Bysshe Shelley was descended. They had three sons.

Robert, the youngest, was born in 1561 or 62 in the old Benedictine priory. The scion of this race which had grown rich by plundering the Church and by unscrupulous time-serving is the mystic among the English martyrs — though circumstances made him a man of action and bold adventure. Fire, sweetness, purity and gentleness were features of Robert Southwell's nature. Few pages in the history of the Reformation and the Counter-Reformation shine so spotlessly as those which bear the names of the English martyrs. They were a motley band — fighters, dreamers, plain, straightforward men of action, converts and born Catholics. But one type is wanting, that of " the politician who pursued his political aims and used religion as a pretext." But there can scarcely be one among those acquainted with this band of heroic saints who has not conceived a peculiar affection for Robert Southwell.

Once, while a child, he was stolen by gipsies — who were numerous in the great woods surrounding St. Faith's. His nurse found him again. As long as he lived Robert Southwell referred at times to this experience of his childhood. "What had I remained with the gipsy? How abject, how void of all knowledge and reverence of God! In what shameful vices, in how great danger of infamy, in how certain danger of an unhappy death and eternal punishment! " On his return to England as a missionary the old nurse was the first person he visited and endeavoured to lead back to the Church.

As a lad he was sent over to Douai and put to school with the Jesuits. It is possible that at this time his father leaned to the old faith — later we know that both he and Robert's brothers adhered to the new system of religion. But of course it is just as likely that his father merely sent the boy to a Jesuit school because such institutions were acknowledged to be the best of their time, and that Richard Southwell reflected that his son might change his religion as easily as other folk, if it was advantageous to do so. Robert took logic together with another young Englishman of good family, John Cotton.

Robert Southwell, however, was inspired with an intense enthusiasm for the Society of Jesus and begged to be received into it at once. He was bitterly disappointed when told that in any case he must be grown up first. But on October 17, 1578, he was received into the Society as a novice; this took place in Rome, and the date according to the old calendar was St Faith's Day.

He was sent for his noviciate to Tournai, but took the vows and was ordained priest in Rome, where for a while he was prefect in the English College. At this time he began to attract a good deal of attention by his poems. He corresponded with Mr. Parsons, the leader of the Jesuit mission in England. In one of his letters he mentions his concern for those at home, who at any rate for a time seem to have practised Catholicism, but had now given way, weary of the everlasting fines and vexations. "Recusants," those who refused to attend the Queen's church, were fined each time they absented themselves from a service. Many of the old families, especially in the country, gentry, farmers and labourers, held out until they were ruined. When they were quite penniless they tried to cross to the Continent and live there on the alms of their co-religionists; the sons enlisted in foreign armies, the daughters went into service or became nuns in one or other of the many English convents abroad. Southwell's letter to Mr. Parsons is couched in covert terms; the outlawed priests were forced to adopt many disguises. Anyone who could assist in the capture of a priest was well rewarded. Mr. Southwell writes:

" Most worthy Sig^r. Eusebius. I am so glad to hear how well Ours have comported themselves, especially he with whom you started. [The allusion is to Edmund Campion's martyrdom.] He has had the start of you in loading his vessel with English wares, and has successfully returned to the desired port. Day by day we are looking forward to hear something similar about you. We hope, however, that the Divine Majesty will not let you leave in such sort as your companion, until you have enriched many with those precious jewels, of which you have taken so large a store to that country.

" One request I particularly make: it is that you would contrive by all possible means to dispose of some of them to the relatives of your friend Robert S [outhwell], for I remember that at one time they were very keen about that particular quality of goods, and kept a factor [? a priest] who was occupied solely in searching for such gems [administering the sacraments]. Possibly, now, after seeing the great losses others have sustained, they may have changed their minds, a circumstance which, if true, would grieve me sorely. . . ."

4

So Robert Southwell knew how in all probability his journey would end, when in 1586 he returned to England to serve as a priest among those Catholics who were still willing to venture life and welfare by hearing a Mass and receiving the Sacraments. Before taking ship in one of the Channel ports he writes to the General of his Order, Claudius Acquaviva, asking for his intercession: " I address you, my Father, from the threshold of death, imploring the aid of your prayers . . . that I may either escape the death of the body for further use, or endure it with courage."

In the towns the majority of the population were now against Catholicism; some had given their adherence to the State church, others belonged to purely Protestant sects, which were also persecuted, but treated with much greater leniency than the Catholics; though no one yet dreamed that the Puritans would one day become a great power in the State. But in the country the greater part of the people still clung to the old faith. It is true that great and justifiable indignation had been felt towards many of the princes of the Church in the former age who had drawn immense incomes from bishoprics and prebends, while leaving the duties of their office to be performed by badly paid vicars. Nor was the conduct

of the parish priests everywhere irreproachable —
though from the evidence which Henry VIII suppressed
and which has since been brought to light it appears
that a great many of them were nevertheless conscientious, clean-living and not unlearned men. A lamentable
case, on the other hand, was that of the so-called Mass-
priests: ordained theologians without a benefice who
made a living as best they could — by saying Masses to
order, undertaking all kinds of scrivener's work, including legal documents, and by teaching children for
payment in kind. The farmers of convent land had grum-
bled at tithes and charges. But if the monks had sometimes clipped them close, their new worldly landlords
flayed them alive. And even when things were at their
worst within the old Church, she had nevertheless performed an immense work in the relief of suffering and
destitution. And this work of charity had been carried
on with a certain tact and good humour: in a Catholic
environment the theoretical respect for people who have
not a stone to rest their head against has always exercised a remarkably healthy check on the tendency of
" benefactors " to feel self-satisfied and to outrage the
human dignity of the receiver; for no one can tell
whether the poor man to whom he offers the gift may
not be just one of the " poor in spirit " of whom Our
Lord speaks, in which case the poor man by his
prayers will bestow an alms on his " benefactor " greater
than can be measured by earthly standards. Now people
no longer thought in this fashion: there was not much
help to be had — in its place the people had been given

the new poor laws which made outlaws of the beggars and crowded the highways with them.

But even in the country-side the band of Catholics who were willing to venture all and endure all for their faith was diminishing. Many more were content to long for better days and to hope that soon there might be another change of religion — they had seen so many. And when they were to die a priest could no doubt be smuggled in to their sick-room to give them the last Sacraments. Among the actively militant, on the other hand, there was a wonderful cohesion and a mutual helpfulness and affection which recalled the days of the primitive Church. But these little congregations who assembled for Mass before dawn in a secret room of some remote manor-house or farm never knew whether a traitor might not be in their midst — whether one of those now kneeling to receive the Holy Communion had already betrayed them, or on going out would give a signal to the priest-hunter. Had not Eliot, who betrayed Edmund Campion in Mrs. Yates's house at Lynford, appeared the most pious and devout at the Communion?

Mr. Southwell found refuge with Lord Vaux of Harrowden, and with his old schoolfellow of Douai, Mr. John Cotton, who had a house in London — one of the Catholics' headquarters. He rode about the country in disguise, saying Mass, hearing confessions, celebrating marriages, baptizing, re-admitting apostates, giving the Sacraments to the dying. He even visited Catholics in prison and said Mass there. For people who had money and could pay their jailers often enjoyed a fair amount of liberty and a good deal of such comfort as was available (and the zeal they showed in obtaining all the benefits they could for their poorer fellow-prisoners is not the least attractive feature in the Catholics of that time). Those on the other hand who were imprisoned "at the public charge" or on whom the persons in power kept a special eye lay rotting in dark and filthy holes and were barely kept from dying of starvation.

A great part of Mr. Southwell's correspondence during these years has been preserved. It gives a lively picture of his adventurous existence; time after time he escaped his pursuers as if by a miracle. Little touches throw light on the conditions prevailing in the circles in which he worked: on one occasion he asks for authority to consecrate chalices and altar-slabs — so much had been taken away in the constant searching of the homes of Catholics that such things had become very scarce. But the Catholics' only consolation is to be able to receive "the bread of Heaven"; if they are deprived of this he is afraid many will "faint and grow feeble, whose piety and constancy was heretofore nourished and increased at this table."

Two letters, to his father and to one of his brothers, Thomas, tell us of his anxiety for his own family. To his father he writes, amongst other things:

"I am not of so unnatural a kind, or of so wild an education, or so unchristian a spirit, as not to remember the root out of which I branched, or to forget my secondary maker and author of my being. It is not the carelessness of a cold affection, nor the want of a due and reverent respect that has made me such a stranger to my native home, and so backward in defraying the debt of a thankful mind, but only the iniquity of these days, that maketh my presence perilous, and the discharge of my duties an occasion of danger. I was loth to enforce an unwilling courtesy upon any. . . ." The letter is very long and full of affectionate prayers that his father may return to the Church before he dies.

To Thomas Southwell he writes: " Shrine not any longer a dead soul in a living body: bail reason out of senses' prison, that after so long a bondage in sin, you may enjoy your former liberty in God's Church, and free your thought from the servile awe of uncertain perils. . . . Weigh with yourself at how easy a price you rate God, Whom you are content to sell for the use of your substance. . . . Look if you can upon a crucifix without blushing; do but count the five wounds of Christ once over without a bleeding conscience."

In any case Robert Southwell succeeded in winning back this brother; in 1590 Thomas Southwell was living in the Netherlands, an exile on account of his faith. After his son's martyrdom old Mr. Southwell died in prison in London, but it is not known whether his imprisonment was due to matters of religion.

After the defeat of the Spanish Armada the position of the English Catholics naturally became even worse. In letter after letter Robert Southwell gives accounts of the martyrdom of his brothers — and often of their wit and humour, of the clear-headedness and presence of mind with which, while undergoing physical and mental torture on the rack and in court, they infuriated their torturers and judges — and very often called forth a kind of reluctant sympathy in a country jury of sport-loving squires and farmers. Rarely had these Catholic priests any prospect worth mentioning of saving their own lives, but they were often able to turn their trial into a defence of the old Faith — and there were always coreligionists whom they were anxious to screen.

Robert Southwell now knew that sooner or later it must be his turn, but he tried to remain at large as long as possible: the more priests were killed or shut up in prison, the more there was to do for those who were yet free. The priests had to adopt disguises and assumed names; Robert Southwell's alias was " Mr. Cotton " — a young man in poor circumstances, rather untidy in his clothes and appearance, fairly awkward when drawn into the conversation of strangers. It seems to have given Edmund Campion some amusement when, disguised as Mr. Edmundes, he tumbled into a Shakespearean tavern scene; with a tankard on the table before him and his rapier across his knees he sat bewitching the whole company with his sparkling humour and the charm of his nature — which his coreligionists were never tired of praising and his enemies could never curse sufficiently: this " seditious Jesuit " charmed all with whom he came in contact. More often than not these casual encounters in roadside inns ended in one or another of his hearers resolving at all costs to continue his acquaintance with Mr. Edmundes — and then Mr. Edmundes led the conversation round to religious questions and finally spoke of " the King," Christ. Campion's words, when he speaks of Christ, ring with a note of chivalry; he is like a knight praising his heroic King. — As to " Mr. Cotton," Robert Southwell says himself that he cut a pretty poor figure at meetings of this kind. And he was not a very promising pupil when his brother in the Order, Mr. Gerard, a mighty sportsman and horseman from his youth in the country, tried to teach him a little sporting slang to use on his travels. Robert Southwell turned this lore to account in his own fashion: in his meditations on the heavenly Lover who seeks for souls he makes use of images from falconry.

About 1590 Robert Southwell became chaplain to Anne, Countess of Arundel. Her husband, the Earl, was a close prisoner in the Tower. — Philip Howard and Anne Dacre were foster-brother and sister and had been married at the age of fourteen. Philip was the son of the Duke of Norfolk who was executed, but some time after the fall of his father Queen Elizabeth took the son into her good graces, and for some years he was one of her favourites. The lad was dazzlingly handsome, a wit after the fashion of the time, one of the best dancers and jousters at court. While Philip spent his time in revels and was involved in one love affair after another, his little wife stayed at home in Arundel House with the old Earl, Philip's grandfather — her young husband swore he would never set eyes on her. One virtue the young lord did have in this wild oats period; he was as extravagant in helping the poor and sick as in everything else. And his servants worshipped him; his manner towards any old washerwoman or beggar was just as courteous and captivating in its gaiety as if she had been a duchess. On the death of his grandfather he became Earl of Arundel and one of the richest noblemen in England. And then he was seized with loathing of the life he had led hitherto. He threw himself into the duties involved by his new position; he received his wife, and before long Lady Anne had succeeded in winning her husband's love entirely.

The captive Edmund Campion had offered to carry on an argument with any one of the Queen's theologians. And in 1583 his challenge was suddenly accepted; an encounter between him and the deans of Windsor and St. Paul's was rapidly arranged in the little church within the walls of the Tower which is dedicated to "St. Peter ad Vincula." Campion was brought there, straight from the rack, into the presence of the Queen and the whole court, who had been summoned to witness this novel form of entertainment. The deans and their assistants were placed in the choir, in arm-chairs, with a great table in front of them covered with bibles and text-books. Campion, who had not received the slightest warning, was still dazed with pain and dull from want of sleep — he was allowed, however, a stool to sit on, and he was told that he was oı 'y to answer questions, not to put any, nor was he allowed any books. The disputation lasted for six hours.

An eyewitness relates: " I heard Mr. Campion reply to the subtleties of his adversaries so easily and so readily, and bear so patiently all the contumely, abuse, derision, and jokes, that the greatest part of the audience, even the heretics who had persecuted him, admired him exceedingly."

Philip Howard was present. He had been present on the day, some months before, when Campion immediately after his capture had been brought before Queen Elizabeth — who received the prisoner with her most amiable smile and offered him the archbishopric of Canterbury if he would retract all he had written as a Catholic and return to her church, whose chief light " Oxford's diamond," " England's Cicero " had once been. The captured Jesuit did homage to the Queen like a courtier, and smilingly thanked Her Grace for her favour, which unfortunately he was unable to accept. His studies had led him to the conviction that the Catholic Church was all it professed to be, the Church which Christ had intended to found. That being so he could not desert it for the newly made church of which Her Grace was the head. . . . Now Philip Howard saw Campion again — his handsome, elegant figure crippled and broken by repeated subjection to torture; Campion was almost paralysed, pale as a corpse, ragged and dirty — but his spirit was as steadfast and cheerful, his mind as brilliantly clear as ever.

Queen Elizabeth soon discovered that the Earl was no longer the same man. Moreover it was reported that he now loved no other women than his wife. But matrimonial happiness was one of the things she did not tolerate in her entourage — with the secret misfortune from which all her so-called "lovers" knew her to suffer, doubtless without any one of them ever finding out what it really was that caused her not to be a normal woman.

At about the same time Lady Anne and the Earl's favourite sister, Lady Margaret Sackville, returned to the Catholic Church. Elizabeth immediately banished the young Countess; she was compelled to reside as a kind of prisoner with a noble family in Surrey, and there she gave birth to her first child, a daughter. Philip was sent to the Tower, but released fairly soon. Then he too went and turned Catholic.

It soon became clear to Philip that England was no place for him. In April 1585 he had made ready to flee across the Channel, but the captain of the ship he had hired betrayed him; he was taken to London and thrown into the Tower again. He was treated so severely in prison that all sorts of guesses were current to explain the Queen's merciless attitude towards her former favourite. All his petitions to be allowed to see his wife and his two children — the son had been born since his father's arrest — were refused. And on various occasions it was reported to his wife that the Earl was drinking in prison, that he had affairs with all kinds of loose women and was entirely indifferent in all that concerned religion. Even when he was at the point of death in 1596 it was made a condition that he must renounce his faith if he would see Anne and the children once before he expired. But in the letters which he contrived to smuggle to Anne from his prison he writes continually

ROBERT SOUTHWELL, S.J.

that it is his sins against her that he regrets most, and
his greatest sorrow is that he will never be able to live
with her again, " for I doubt not but you should have
found me as good a husband to my poor ability by God's
Grace, as you have found me bad heretofore."

And to Robert Southwell Arundel writes:

" I call Our Lord to witness that as no sin grieves me
so much as my offences to that party [Anne], so no
worldly thing makes me loather to depart hence than
that I cannot live to make that party satisfaction, according to my most ardent and affectionate desire. Afflictio
dat intellectum (affliction gives understanding) ."

During the time Mr. Southwell was concealed in
Arundel House in London he corresponded with the
Earl. Besides the faith which united them they had the
common bond of being poets. The Earl was no great
poet, though there are graceful and feeling lines among
his verses. And the translations he made during his imprisonment are clear and tasteful. Amongst other works
he translated Lanspergius' " Epistle of Jesus Christ " — a
book of devotion which has been reprinted many times
in the course of the years, most recently in " The Or-
chard Series." [1]

Robert Southwell's religious poems, on the other
hand, have always had their little band of fire-worship-
pers, among Protestants as well as Catholics — some of
them are to be found in most English anthologies, but
no entirely satisfactory edition of them is yet available,

[1] Published by Burns, Oates & Washbourne, London; Benziger
Brothers, New York.

so far as I know. Ben Johnson remarked to Drummond that "Southwell was hanged, yet so he [Jonson] had written that piece of his 'The Burning Babe' he would have been content to destroy many of his."

Many of the poems were composed while he lived in hiding at Arundel House. Lady Anne had installed a private printing press there, and Southwell wrote a number of apologetic and controversial pamphlets and devotional books in prose, which were printed in the house. But in his secret chamber of the great mansion he was able for the first time since his return from Rome to be absorbed in meditation. For a little while the contemplative mystic that dwelt within him came into his own. In his poems it is above all the mystery of Christmas that occupies his thoughts. Circumstances had made him a cavalry leader in the militia of Jesus Christ, as one of his fellows calls himself. Now the soldier was permitted for a short time to kneel before the manger and do homage to his King in His childish grace and helpless littleness. " A Childe my Choyse," " New Prince, New Pompe," "New Heaven, New Warre," " The Burning Babe " and many more poems on the Child Jesus and His Mother are written in the figurative language of the Elizabethan age, and he has the passionate love of a man of the Renaissance for similes which at times are rather artificial. But his Christmas poems have a dark golden lustre of their own. And there is an unforgettable power in his image of Christ — the eternal God who unwearied through all eternity supports the earth on His finger-tip and encloses all creation in the hollow of His hand — but in His humanity breaks down and falls beneath the weight of a single person's sin. And his vision of the Child Jesus appearing as a blazing meteor over the frozen fields of earth — as a ball of fire from the glowing love which is the primal element behind all things created — is strange and startling in the interplay of its Renaissance extravagance, the naturalism of its imagery and the unrestrained passion of its feeling. His last and simpler poems from the time of his imprisonment are eloquent of his longing to complete his course and to be brought where he can see the Beloved face to face.

5

MR. SOUTHWELL had frequently said Mass at Uxenden Hall, Harrow on the Hill, the house of Mr. Richard Bellamy. The Bellamy family was known for its fidelity to the old religion and had paid the full price of it, year after year.

At this time Richard Topcliffe was one of the best known and most notorious of the Government's agents in the hunting of priests. As we have seen, torture was customary at the time in most courts of justice, whether in religious or other causes. I saw that Kristian Schjelderup (in a recent article on psycho-analysis) surmises that the use of torture by the Spanish Inquisition was probably due to the ascetic judges having suffered from repressed instincts which inclined them to sadism. This

appears to me to betray a somewhat limited knowledge
of history. Torture has been employed against enemies
— for political objects or for the sake of amusement —
by Oriental and European despots who never dreamed
of suppressing any of their appetites in any direction,
and by models of civic virtue who led an exemplary
family life with their own wedded wives and were the
most affectionate of fathers to their own offspring —
elaborate torture of prisoners has been the practice
among savages who enforced a rigorous sexual morality
within the tribe, as well as among peoples who to all
appearance were not troubled with any sexual morality.
— Topcliffe seems actually to have been a sadist — it
appears that he derived keen enjoyment from examining
people " straytly." On the other hand he could not in
any way be called an ascetic: in his generosity to himself he amassed houses and estates, women, wine, titles
and all else that the age reckoned among the good things
of life. In the end his greediness brought about his fall
— scandal reported that at last he came to regard himself as so irresistible a seducer that he imagined the
Queen herself had cast eyes on him. More probably it
was others who had cast their eyes on some of the prop-
erties he had acquired, in reward for such work as the
detection of Anthony Babington's conspiracy. It would
be interesting to know what instincts Richard Topcliffe
can have suppressed in himself. —

Anne Bellamy of Uxenden Hall was imprisoned at
the instance of the Bishop of London in The Gatehouse,
a remnant of the old Benedictine Abbey of Westmin-

ster which was still standing. This was in January 1592. While in prison Anne Bellamy became pregnant, and there was at any rate a report that Topcliffe himself had violated her. It is at least certain that from this time forth she was in his power and he used her as his tool and agent.

Doubtless on account of her pregnancy Anne was released and allowed to lodge with a family in Holborn, where she was kept under strict supervision. While there she succeeded in getting into communication with Mr. Southwell, who had been her confessor; it is alleged in contemporary letters that she got him to come to her, that he received her confession and gave her absolution. In that case it must have been on this occasion that Mr. Southwell told Anne that he was to celebrate Mass in her home, Uxenden, on Sunday, June 20, 1592. Accordingly Anne warned Mr. Topcliffe.

In any case it is certain that Mr. Topcliffe had on him a letter written in Anne Bellamy's hand and a sketch of the house on which the secret chamber was marked, when early in the morning of that Sunday he appeared at Uxenden Hall accompanied by Judge Barnes and a posse of men and surrounded the house. Mr. Bellamy was not at home, but Mrs. Bellamy made an attempt to deny that they had a priest in the house. Mr. Topcliffe produced her daughter's letter, and Robert Southwell was arrested, while still wearing his vestments. He was put on a horse, the altar requisites, Papist images and books and whatever else they could find in the way of booty were loaded on a cart. By six o'clock the same morning Topcliffe had his prisoner safely housed in his own dwelling at Westminster.

Southwell was instantly subjected to torture — hung up by the wrists against a wall, so that he could barely touch the floor with the tips of his toes. Those who have not tried it can have no idea of what an intolerable agony this is, writes another of the priests of this time — one who had himself tried it several times, but escaped in the end. Southwell was left hanging almost without intermission for two days and nights; only when it looked as if he were about to die did they take him down and hold burning paper under his nose — then he came to himself, vomited blood, and they hung him up again. What they particularly wished him to disclose was whether he knew Lady Arundel, and whether he could give the names of other priests who were in the country. Mr. Southwell acknowledged that he was a priest and a Jesuit, but beyond that they could not get a word out of him — he would not even tell the colour of the horse he had ridden to Uxenden; he was afraid it might lead to the detection of the horse's owner. Even Sir Robert Cecil, the Treasurer, who was present, was impressed by the prisoner's unshakable endurance, and one or two of the executioner's assistants began to whisper that this man must indeed be a saint. All he uttered, from time to time, was: " My God and my all! God gave Himself to thee; give thyself to God! "

Nevertheless Mr. Topcliffe wrote with his own hand to the Queen herself (the letter is still in existence) , describing his proceedings in the case of Mr. Southwell in detail: " I did never take so weighty a man; if he be rightly used."

From Topcliffe's house Robert Southwell was taken across to the Gatehouse and put into a cell so foul that when he was brought out again after a month or so his clothes were covered with lice. His father then made an application to the Queen, humbly praying " that if his son had committed anything for which by the laws he deserved death, he might suffer death; if not, as he was a gentleman, he hoped her Majesty would be pleased to order that he should be treated as a gentleman, and not be confined any longer in that filthy hole." The Queen granted Mr. Richard Southwell's request and gave orders that the Jesuit Southwell should be transferred to better quarters in the prison. His father was permitted to send him clothes and other necessaries, among them such books as he desired. Robert Southwell then asked to have the Bible and the writings of St. Bernard.

Topcliffe had promised Anne Bellamy that none of her family should suffer for having housed the priest. He did not keep his promise however; Anne's father and mother, two sisters and two brothers were taken to various prisons and " examined straytly." Topcliffe was specially anxious to break the spirit of old Mrs. Bellamy —" the old hen that hatched the chicks (the worst that ever was) ," he writes of her. Mrs. Bellamy died in prison. One of the sons renounced his faith, the rest of her children remained unswervingly constant. Topcliffe married Anne Bellamy to one of his under-jailers. Her father had been released, since he had not been at home on the morning when Southwell said Mass in his house; but now Topcliffe had him imprisoned again for refusing to pay Anne's husband the dowry promised him by Topcliffe. Mr. Bellamy however regained his freedom in the end and died in Belgium.

Robert Southwell was removed to the Tower and kept a prisoner there for nearly three years. During this time he was subjected to torture on at least thirteen occasions — such is the number of which Cecil had knowledge.

Many of his beautiful poems on death, the good death that is to tear away the last veil that parts him from God, were composed in prison. His long poem, " St. Peter's Complaint," also belongs to this time. It contains some of Southwell's most beautiful verses.

Not once was he given an opportunity of confessing or saying Mass. And it is unlikely that he was allowed to receive any visits, except a single one from his sister. But it happened occasionally that some of his faithful friends gained admission to the gardens of the Tower — the functionaries' wives were allowed to sell flowers and vegetables from their patches of garden. Their customers might then have a glimpse of Mr. Southwell at a window and receive his blessing from afar. Arundel and Southwell were never allowed to meet, but now and again a note was smuggled from one to the other, and sometimes Arundel's dog followed the turnkey into Southwell's cell. The Lieutenant of the Tower rallied Arundel about this, saying he supposed the dog had

gone to get the priest's blessing. The Earl laughed:
" Marry! it is no news for irrational creatures to seek
blessings at the hands of holy men. St. Jerome writes
how those lions which had digged with their paws St.
Paul the Hermit's grave stood after waiting with their
eyes upon St. Anthony expecting his blessing."

At last Southwell sent a letter to the all-powerful
Cecil, humbly entreating that " he might either be
brought to trial, to answer for himself, or at least that
his friends might have leave to come and see him."
Cecil answered that " if he was in so much haste to be
hanged, he should quickly have his desire." Shortly
afterwards he was taken from the Tower to Newgate
prison and placed in an underground dungeon that
went by the name of Limbo. And three days later, on
February 20, 1595, he was brought to the bar at Westminster.

The indictment was one of treason, charging Robert
Southwell, clerk, last domiciled in London, a born subject of the Queen, with having received priest's orders
contrary to the law of the land from the pretended authority of the See of Rome. Then followed further state-
ments of his activities, his arrest, and so on.

Mr. Southwell was driven forward to the bar at point
of halberd, his hands tied behind his back. The court
was crowded with spectators. Then Southwell's hands
were freed; he took off his hat and saluted the judges
with a deep bow. He was a tall man, rather slight, with
light brown hair and beard — his worn white face still
had a quite boyish look. The Lord Chief Justice asked

how old he was. Mr. Southwell replied that he was "about the same age as our Saviour, namely thirty-three." Topcliffe, who was present, cried out charging him with insupportable pride in comparing himself with the Saviour. Mr. Southwell answered that he had not meant it so; he knew well that he was a worm of the earth, and the work and creature of Christ his Maker.

To the question, guilty or not guilty, Mr. Southwell replied that he acknowledged himself to be her Majesty's subject, and that by authority from God, by the means of the Church of Rome, he was a Catholic priest (he did thank God for it) , and that he was at Uxenden on the day he was arrested, he could not deny. But he had never plotted against her Majesty's sovereignty and had returned to his native land with no other object than that of administering the Sacraments according to the rites of the Holy Church to all who desired them.

He was interrupted — he was only to answer the question, guilty or not guilty. Southwell then answered: "Not guilty of any treason."

Thereupon he was asked by whom he would be judged. " By God and by you, my lords."

The Lord Chief Justice said No, he must answer, by God and his country. Southwell objected to using this form. In this point the law of his country was in conflict with the law of God, "and he was loth those ˙or men the jurors should be accessory or guilty to his death." However, he had to submit to the finding of the jury, which was of course: guilty.

On being questioned whether he had anything more to

say in his defence, he shook his head: " Nothing; but from my heart I beg of Almighty God to forgive all who have been any ways accessory to my death."

Lord Chief Justice Popham bade him see to his soul's welfare while there was yet time; Southwell replied that he had done so long ago. He declined with thanks the offer of a minister of the established church to prepare him — the grace of God would be more than sufficient for him. When sentence of death had been solemnly pronounced — that he should be hanged as a traitor, but cut down before life was extinct, and so on; all the ghastly details — he saluted the court with a deep bow and expressed his thanks for the favour shown him.

He was taken back to Newgate, and people stood closely packed in the streets through which he was to pass. And once more they marvelled at these extraordinary Papist priests — Robert Southwell too shone as he walked, as though his whole being were filled with felicity at the prospect of being executed on the morrow.

He spent his last night in Limbo. And early next morning Southwell was led out and placed on a hurdle, harnessed with two horses that were to draw him to Tyburn. The authorities had done their best to prevent its being known on what day the celebrated Mr. Southwell's execution should take place, but it had been rumoured in spite of them. A crowd of people poured towards the place of execution, among them " many persons of high rank." — For Southwell was also a famous poet and belonged to a family of note.

The celebrated " Tyburn Tree " was a gallows of the

type that can still be seen outside Visby, where on the old gallows hill three tall pillars of masonry are still standing. These supported a triangle of beams. In England at any rate the culprit who was to be hanged was placed in a cart which was driven underneath the gallows. The hangman sat on the beam above, his assistants stood by the condemned man in the cart and placed the rope about his neck. Then the cart was driven from under him and he was left hanging — till he was dead, or fit to be cut down, according to his sentence.

When Mr. Southwell stood in the cart he made the sign of the cross as well as he could with his tied hands and began to preach to the people on the words of the Apostle in the Epistle to the Romans, fourteenth chapter: "Whether we live, we live unto the Lord: or whether we die, we die unto the Lord. Therefore, whether we live or whether we die, we are the Lord's."

The sheriff would have stopped him, but Mr. Southwell asked leave to say a few words more — he would speak nothing offensive. (How much a condemned man was allowed to say in his last moments depended above all on the feeling around him; some were shouted down at once, others were allowed to make long speeches or sermons before the cart was drawn from under them.) "I am brought hither to perform the last act of this miserable life, and . . . I do most humbly desire at the hands of Almighty God for our Saviour Jesus' sake, that He would vouchsafe to pardon and forgive all my sins. . . ." He acknowledged that he was a Catholic priest and a Jesuit, declared that he had never intended harm or evil against the Queen, but had always prayed for her, and he prayed for her now, commended his poor country into the hands of Almighty God, and finally prayed that his death might be for his own good and that of his country and a consolation to his Catholic brethren. Then he crossed himself again and prayed: " In manus tuas, Domine — into Thy hands, Lord, I commend my spirit." At that moment the cart was jerked away.

The hangman was an awkward beginner, and he had arranged the noose so clumsily about Robert Southwell's neck that he hung for a good while before losing consciousness. Three or four times he was seen to raise his hands in an attempt to make the sign of the cross. Then someone ran forward, seized his legs and pulled to put an end to his torment. And when the hangman seemed about to cut him down before he was dead, there were angry cries from many quarters: " Stay, stay! " The crowd insisted that this Jesuit should be left hanging till he was dead — they had liked him so well as he stood in the cart.

So he was already a corpse when he was cut down and quartered.

On the same day Mr. Garnet wrote to the General of the Order giving an account — in the flowery style of the time — of Southwell's execution:

" Behold, now at length I present to his Paternity a lovely flower gathered from his gardens, the sweetest fruit from his tree, a priceless treasure from his bank, silver weighed, tried and seven-fold purged from earthly dross in the fire; an invincible soldier, a most faithful disciple and courageous martyr of Christ, Robert Southwell, my former most beloved companion and brother, now my patron, a king reigning together with Christ."

Less than a year later Philip Howard died in his prison. His body was wrapped in a sheet, laid in a plain coffin and buried without any ceremony under the floor of the little church of St. Peter ad Vincula, where fourteen years before he had listened to Edmund Campion defending his Faith. There is not much resemblance between the portrait of Philip at seventeen — the face of a charming youth, still rather childish in its rounded softness, with great beaming eyes, full red lips and brown curly hair, radiant with overweening youth, pride and refined sensuousness — and the picture of the imprisoned Earl which is said to have been painted by one of the officers of the Tower; here the bony structure of the wasted face is sharply prominent, the eyes seem to have grown smaller under their tired lids, the lips have narrowed and are half concealed by a thin and straggling growth of beard. Only the rather large, long nose and the very finely drawn eyebrows are the same. But Philip Howard too thanked God, as he lay dying.

It was said that he died of poison, naturally. The cause of death appears to have been miliary tuberculosis. He had been given a promise that he would be allowed to see his wife and children, if he would abjure his faith, and Philip Howard replied that he could not do that.

Twenty-nine years after his death Lady Anne and his

son received permission from King James I to remove Philip Howard's body to the chapel in Arundel Castle.

Lady Anne lived until 1630. When her little daughter died, at the age of fifteen, her mother said to a cousin: " Ah, my Bess is gone to heaven, and if it were Almighty God's Will, I wish the other were as well gone after her! " " The other " was her son. With him she went through a repetition of his father's story — he turned out ambitious and a libertine, and deserted the faith of his fathers. And when at last he returned to it, his mother was dead. Through all the years of her widowhood her life was entirely devoted to prayer and good works. One of her friends relates how on the birthdays of her grandchildren she always had all the poor children of the neighbourhood brought up to the castle. They were entertained at a dinner composed of all the good things children like best. Before leaving each received a gift of money, and finally they were shown into the room where the invalid lady lay and given a big slice of cake from the dish that stood by her bed.

Anne Dacre now lies beside her husband in the chapel at Arundel. This chapel (formerly the chancel of the parish church) is the property of the Catholic Duke of Norfolk, and the tomb of the Venerable Philip Howard is visited every year by pilgrims from every part of England.

The railings on the north side of Hyde Park now run where was once the place of execution outside London, and close by, in Hyde Park Place, there is a little convent of Benedictine nuns, where the Sacrament is exposed for adoration day and night all through the year.

One early morning in May I climbed down from the bus at the Marble Arch and asked a tall and fresh-complexioned young policeman the way to Tyburn Convent. The man was obviously a Catholic and no doubt an Irishman. "What about Tyburn Tree? — I expect you want to see that too, the place where the gallows stood — *that's* where you ought to begin, you know, ma'am." He evidently took it for granted that a lady who was looking for Tyburn Convent had come out with the object of performing some kind of devotion. So he showed me where I could find the spot which he considered the most suitable point of departure.

Close by, at the crossing where Edgware Road comes in from the north, a little bronze triangle has been let into the roadway. Three paces from it is a refuge, where one can escape the stream of traffic and wait to cross the street.

Cars whizzed past and the heavy red omnibuses swung round from Edgware Road. On the other side the park's sea of foliage lay in the morning sunlight behind the white Marble Arch. It was strange to be standing there — a strange place in which to make one's devotions. But Our Lord's world is strange in many ways, for that matter — .

Afterwards I went on to Tyburn Convent, where the monstrance shines above the little altar, waiting for people who come in from Park Lane or from other quarters of the world — .

MARGARET CLITHEROW

A CHRISTMAS story ought to have a happy ending — at any rate if it is intended for a Christmas number.[1] The story may be as exciting as you please, the heroine may be exposed to perilous situations and terrible sufferings before the reassuring conclusion is reached. Emotional readers may be allowed to shed a few tears, but they are to feel sure all the time that it *must* end happily: at last all difficulties are resolved in joy and gladness — preferably of course it ought to end in something like an engagement or a wedding or a Christmas party with friends who meet again after many adventures and a long separation. Besides this the story ought in one way or another to glorify the home and mutual affection between parents and children, and it must end with the prospect of some people living happily ever after " and if they haven't died they're still alive."

I have also got the idea that a story for an annual of

any kind ought to take place in England and the people in it ought to have English names. Very well then — we Catholics have some exciting stories to tell of noble ladies and brave gentlemen who lived in England and had genuine English names. They are rather different from the usual "magazine stuff," but that is because they really happened.

All things considered, the story of Margaret Clitherow seems to me quite suitable for a Christmas annual, even if I merely recapitulate what her contemporaries tell us about her. Most of the information comes from people who knew the worthy butcher Clitherow's young wife and sent in their notes to the men who in the days of the Protestant inquisition were collecting material for the Church's heroic saga in England.

When the Catholics of England at the present time ask that the sanctity of the English martyrs may soon be proclaimed to the Catholic Church all over the world, it is not, of course, with the intention of digging up every old document that can be produced in retaliation for the old tales, historical and legendary, of the Spanish Inquisition and the fires of Smithfield. There would be little excuse for us Catholics if we took to writing history on these lines — selecting isolated events which happened five or three hundred years ago, tearing them out of their environment and judging them in the light of ideas and conceptions which are the product of the last century's mentality. What the Church desires is that we remember the martyrs as intercessors and patterns. Their executioners and the laws which brought them to martyrdom are only of interest in so far as they were instruments. But in addition this little group of the " white-robed army of martyrs " — the English martyrs — has a special interest for us from a purely human point of view.

Born and bred in the period which school-books call the Renaissance, their attitude to the newest and most vigorous fancies and superstitions of their time was surprisingly free and unprejudiced; and this is in reality a far more difficult matter than liberating oneself from ancient, mummified prejudices and superstitions. They had seen the new-born bantlings of the " rebirth " in their cradle, surrounded by delighted parents and aunts and sponsors, and without allowing themselves to be distracted by the enthusiasm of its progenitors they had predicted what the child would be like when it grew up. For us who live in the golden age of opportunism they may serve as patterns by their faithfulness until death, by the meekness and strength which enabled them to pass their lives in ceaseless prayer and mental composure — in the dungeon's hell, on the rack and beneath the gallows. They knew what they counted as supremely valuable and did not allow themselves to be disturbed by the cares and temptations of " this world," nor by a love of this world's most real and excellent good things — for which reason it is natural that so many have chosen them as patrons in our time, when cares and temptations of an extremely real nature would be a hard enough strain on the will-power and coolness of most people — and when we nevertheless fritter away our faculties and allow the splinters of our personality to be scattered by trivialities. And the fresh sportsman-like spirit which the English martyrs preserved while playing hide-and-seek with death day after day, the ready wit that many of these young priests and laymen could command even with the rope about their necks and the hangman's knives and braziers before their eyes — these ought to appeal to everything that impels us to hero-worship. If these men and women had gone to their death for a purely worldly cause it is fairly certain that their story would be known to many more; it would have been retold for the edification of brave boys and girls — school-books and popular illustrated works would have extolled their courage and chivalry and cheerful contempt of death, if they had died for some other cause than the unity of the Church of Christ and the supremacy of the spiritual life over the changing forms of worldly society, and if their last words had been something different and more popular than the name of Jesus.

Of course the death to which they were condemned was not a torture specially invented for Catholics. In most European countries death at the stake was the punishment for heinous attacks on the security of society: so it was in Spain, when the Inquisition had declared a man an incorrigible heretic, the law of the land ranked heresy as treason against society, and now it stepped in. So it was in Norway, when the woman who claimed to be Eirik Magnusson's daughter, " the Maid of Norway," was burnt at Nordnes in 1301. And according to some authorities Agmund Sigurdsson Bolt, who in 1436 led the revolt against foreign officials in Norway, is said to have attempted a fresh rebellion some years later which ended in his being burnt.

In England traitors were hanged on a gallows, but cut down before losing consciousness; they were then ripped up and the hangman groped about among the entrails till he got hold of the heart — then he tore it out, showed it to the people and threw it on the fire. Under Elizabeth's grandfather, the first of the Tudor kings, this mode of execution had been carried out on the young Earl of Warwick, last male descendant of the House of Plantagenet; and together with him Henry VII caused to be executed the handsome and chivalrous young pretender who gave himself out to be one of the two little sons of Edward IV — whom Richard III was supposed to have had murdered in the Tower. Margaret of Burgundy had acknowledged him as her nephew, several of Edward IV's closest friends alleged that they recognized Prince Richard of York — which in itself need mean no more than a desire to be rid of the Tudor. However, the Tudor won the day, and the young man passed into history as what the Tudor party declared him to be — a certain Perkin Warbeck, son of a ferryman at Tournai.

The Protestants, of course, asserted from the outset that they did not intend to exercise any restraint of conscience, so it was made an act of treason to adhere to the Catholic Church — " the Old Religion," as it was then called. Therefore a long, long line of Catholic priests and laymen died under Elizabeth and her successors, as traitors, for refusing to betray their faith.

" And after that they lived long and happily, and if they are not dead they are living yet." For as St. Paul once wrote to the good people of Corinth: " And if Christ be not risen again, then is our preaching vain: and your faith is also vain."

But if I have chosen Margaret Clitherow as the subject of a Christmas story, and not any other of the English martyrs, it is because her story ends with the final reunion of a mother and her children. Besides which Margaret looks so charming in the existing portrait of her — with irregular, intelligent and delicate features surrounded by the becoming matron's coif of those days, a broad and open forehead, finely drawn eyebrows and a sweet little mouth. A reflection of the young woman's gentle dignity and cheerful fortitude shines in the old accounts of Mistress Clitherow's life and death. All those who were occupied with her case would have preferred to spare her — personally she appears to have had none but friends. And then she of all people was to remain faithful to a persecuted and hated religion in the midst of every terror. Here is her story.

Her father's name was Middleton; he was a wealthy and respected citizen of the rich and ancient city of York. The halls of craftsmen's and merchants' guilds occupy as much room as the many handsome parish churches in the narrow and winding streets of York. Traffic was lively in yards and alleys, and the open

squares were filled with busy marketing, for York serves
a large tract of country and the city was the centre of the
wool trade and of cattle-raising and dairy products —
York hams and beef and cheeses and Yorkshire pudding
have been famous for centuries. Assizes were held here;
the gentry from the country round had their town
houses and journeyed to and fro on handsome horses
or in picturesque lumbering coaches.

But above all York had been an ecclesiastical centre
ever since Pope Gregory the Great decided that St.
Paulinus, the apostle of Northumbria, should have his
archiepiscopal see here. In the time of the Romans York
— Eboracum — had been one of the most important
towns in the province of Britannia. A tradition asserts
that Constantine the Great was born here; in any case
it is certain that here he was proclaimed Roman Emperor. The city can show remains of many buildings of
the Roman period, among them the traces of Christian
churches, and its museum contains several tombstones
of Christian Romans. And a Bishop of Eboracum is
mentioned among the Bishops from Britain who attended the Council of Arles in 314. Then nothing is
known of the city's history from the time when the
Romans withdrew the last of their troops from the province in 410 until St. Paulinus in 627 baptized King
Edwin here. St. Paulinus was beginning afresh in a country entirely heathen when he erected the first church of
St. Peter on the rising ground above the River Ouse.
It was no doubt a little wooden church; it was replaced,
first by a Saxon, then by a Norman, church of stone, and

finally in 1230 the erection of the beautiful Gothic cathedral which still stands was commenced. The building was completed in the course of 250 years — it is the greatest of England's cathedrals and one of the finest, and it has preserved more of its splendid mediæval stained glass than any other church in England. Several of the parish churches also contain old glass, so that a visit to York is necessary in order to form an idea of old English stained glass.

The quarter containing the Minster and the Archbishop's palace was surrounded by a wall of its own, and " the Liberty of St. Peter " had its own jurisdiction and privileges. Outside it lay the city with its girdle of walls, gates, barbicans, bastions and towers, and within the fortified area the towers and spires of parish churches and hospitals and hostels and convents and schools with their own chapels rose high above the clustered houses, so that all day long the choir of bells rang out over the swarming life in the network of streets. Outside the city walls again stood a great Benedictine abbey, and this too had a wall surrounding its precincts. With all these different walls enclosing and adjoining one another the city must have resembled a piece of honeycomb with its separate cells.

There is still enough left of old York to make the city what the guide-books call " a pearl." The city walls are standing, so that one can walk along the parapet all round, looking down into the mediæval quarters and the old gardens of the former Liberty of St. Peter, and getting a comprehensive view of the cathedral's mighty

masses of towers and roofs and flying buttresses and
gables towards every point of the compass.

Some years after the birth of Margaret Middleton the
faith of St. Paulinus had been banned and Queen Elizabeth had introduced a new religion which the people
were bound under penalty to profess — and the system
of penalties gradually became as comprehensive in es-
sentials as it was precise in details. It was penal to
take part in services other than those prescribed in the
Queen's name; it was penal to absent oneself from these;
penal to have received Catholic ordination; penal to
" harbour, maintain or aid " a Catholic priest. To the
See of York the Queen — " Pope Elizabeth," as a flippant young priest called her in court — had appointed
her own subservient bishop and clergy. The monks and
nuns had been driven out long before; their property
had been confiscated and for the most part had come
into the hands of the new plutocracy; it was inadvisable
to retain any memory of them beyond the scandals, true
and untrue, which were told about the convents; a great
part of their libraries was well preserved under the
counters of hucksters and in the warehouses of wool-
staplers: parchment is a strong material for packing,
and for that purpose there is no danger in its being inscribed with Latin prayers or painted with miniatures
of the life of Christ or the story of His Mother.

Margaret Middleton's parents had embraced the
Queen's religion — it was in fact pre-eminently the re-
ligion of rich and enterprising citizens. In 1571, when
Margaret was seventeen, Master Middleton gave his

daughter to Master Clitherow's son John, an honest and reputable butcher, and the young people moved into a house in The Shambles, the butchers' quarter. The Clitherow family had not conformed so unconditionally to the new religion — there is mention of a son who was a priest — but Margaret's bridegroom had yielded, outwardly at any rate, and passed as a Protestant. But it may be that at times in any case he had in his heart more sympathy for the old Faith. He was an honourable man, kind and generous, his pretty young wife loved and admired him — and then came the children; Margaret had three. The eldest, Henry, appeared predestined to continue the family traditions and become a citizen butcher of the good city of York. Then came a little girl, Anne, and another boy. Perhaps even before the birth of her youngest child the mother had taken the fateful step. Young Mistress Clitherow was no doubt living in clover, as they say. And then a few years after her marriage she must needs get herself received into the persecuted Church.

It would be unjust to forget that Master John Clitherow was much to be pitied. We only know how he acted, we know nothing of how he thought and felt about all that happened in the years between his wife's conversion and her death. In marrying this rich and charming, well brought-up Protestant maiden he cannot possibly have dreamed that one day she was destined for her conscience' sake to bring tragedy into their peaceful home. John Clitherow cannot have been prepared, any more than others, to see the fulfilment of Our Lord's terrible words about the sword which He came to bring, in his own house in Little Shambles, York, or that of all others his sweet and hearty little Margaret should be called to testify with her blood to a love of Christ which was stronger even than her love of her husband and children.

Perhaps after all John Clitherow never thought it would go so far as this. Margaret was the first *woman* to suffer martyrdom under the laws against the adherents of the old Faith. It is surely not unlikely that this citizen of a rich English Renaissance town in Shakespeare's time thought to himself: what! *kill* a woman, my wife, they won't do that — !

Mistress Clitherow was no scholar — she only learned to read and write during one of her periods of imprisonment. But it is reported of her that " all her actions were tempered with all inward tranquillity and comfort, with mild and smiling countenance; ready of tongue, but yet her words modest, and courteous, and lowly; quick in the despatch of business, and then most pleasant when she could the most serve God, or procure the same to others."

Her replies under examination show that she was able to support her faith by purely intellectual arguments and to correct the various Protestant clergymen's erroneous assertions regarding Catholic dogmas and Catholic practice. And from her earliest youth she had spent much time in prayer and had thought upon God with profound love and great reverence. Honestly and without any consideration of worldly advantage or peace she had prayed for light, that she might be able to distinguish which faith was the true one. When she felt sure that she knew this, she acted without fear or wavering.

The enemies of the Catholic Church have always directed their attacks in the first place against the sacrifice of the Mass and the Sacrament of the Altar. From the time of the Roman Emperors to that of Mexican Presidents the mode of proceeding has always been the same — an attempt to strike at the Church in the most central point of her life. By persecution, terror, ruin, ridicule, by any and every means, it has been sought to keep the flock of the faithful away from the Mass and the Sacraments — and the object is that the flock shall shrink until it looks no more imposing than a scraped-up handful of Christian folk in the middle of the arena of a great amphitheatre. Each time Catholicism has been vanquished, just so far as it can be vanquished by men.

Margaret obtained her husband's permission to install a chapel in their home and to house and assist the outlawed priests who roamed about the country, disguised and in danger of their lives every hour of the day. What kind of men were they? Young noblemen and peasant lads who faced death for the faith they had been taught on their mothers' knees; young sons of the new well-to-do middle class who had studied theology in the Protestant universities with the result that they became Catholics; clergymen of the new established church who already possessed a Protestant benefice when they received the call to tend and serve a scattered flock, with

no home and no hope of other reward than martyrdom.
They travelled secretly all over the country, comforted
the dying, reconciled the apostates, strengthened the
terrified — in some hidden chamber of a Catholic home
they said Mass before daybreak, administering the Sacrament to the little band of hungry souls who furtively
met there. There was always the danger that a Judas
might be among them — denunciation of Catholics had
become a common and profitable profession in England.
It was not unknown for parents to denounce their children and children their parents. Particularly dangerous
was it for Catholics to receive the poor and homeless
who begged for help — this was a trick the spies frequently practised with success. More than one priest was
arrested while he stood before the altar, and taken by
the shortest road to martyrdom.

Many of the priests who died at York's Tyburn — the
place of execution here bore the same well-known name
as that outside London — had said Mass in Margaret's
house. At these services the mistress of the house always
knelt nearest the door, on guard, listening for any warning sound. At the same time she followed with burning
intensity the holy act which was accomplished on the
altar. During the offertory, when the priest " in the spirit
of humility and with a contrite heart " raised the wine
and the bread and prayed that they might become for us
the Body and Blood of Jesus, her most intimate friends
tell us that Margaret would offer herself as a sacrifice,
praying that she too, through the grace of the Holy
Spirit, might be made of like nature with Christ.

Then there were long intervals when she had to do without the Mass and the Sacraments. She was always up an hour or two before the rest of the household were awake, praying alone in the empty room which served as chapel. All through the day she performed the innumerable tasks which fell upon the mistress of a great middle-class household towards the end of the sixteenth century. " A good wife, a tender mother, a kind mistress, loving God above all things and her neighbour as herself," it was said of her. By the sweetness of her nature she bore witness to the charm of piety. " The best wife in all England," her husband lamented, when he had lost her.

But sometimes she went out at night. Together with a few other Catholic women she walked barefoot, praying all the way, to the place of execution where for her and her friends the earth was soaked with the blood of saints. These pilgrimages gave them courage to face the troubles and dangers of every day and all the difficulties which were the daily bread of them all.

The Protestant Archbishop of York, Dr. Grindall, made serious representations to Queen Elizabeth. In his diocese alone an uncomfortably large proportion of the population openly defied the principle of the Reformation: that it is the sovereign who decides what the people are to believe. In Northern England the Protestants were absolutely in a minority: besides all those who did not attend Protestant services and made no secret of being Catholics, large sections of the population clung to the Church in their hearts and sympathized with their more courageous fellows who dared to fight for the Faith.

A tribunal was therefore established with the object of tracking down and extirpating priests and terrorizing laymen from housing them and taking part in the Mass.

Margaret was suspected. Margaret was imprisoned. At one time she was kept in prison for over two years. She was confined in a filthy, cold, dark hole, on the poorest prison fare, separated from her dear ones. She herself refers to this time as " a happy and profitable school "; here she learned to be patient, to live with God in solitude. And here no one could be inconvenienced by her fasting and practising all kinds of self-denial (in addition to the punishment of imprisonment!). Love needs to express itself in outward signs and acts, and for one kind of love it is just as natural to mark one's own flesh with stripes as it is for another kind of love to carve hearts and initials on benches and the trunks of trees. According to human estimation Margaret's life was blameless and unstained. But she herself was overwhelmed by her own nothingness and the frailty of her nature, the more she became familiar with God and the more she received of the light and warmth of His love.

In those periods when she was at liberty it often happened that people who had themselves submitted to the Queen's ecclesiastical laws gave Margaret warning when there was a danger of her house being searched. They thought that was the least they could do for a person who had never asked any questions about religion or worthiness when she was able to help anyone with en-

couragement or money. And if Margaret heard of anyone who had used incautious speech that might expose
her co-religionists to danger, she was never afraid to go
to them and beg them to be more careful. Evidently no
one found it easy to say no to Mistress Clitherow.

The spies kept watch on her house; but Margaret
hired a room in another part of the city, where the
Catholics could meet for Mass. As things were, she herself was seldom able to be present: but, she said, "my
heart is with you, and I trust you remember me when I
am toiling in the world. And though I cannot come as
I desire, yet it doth me good and much comforteth me
that I know I have you here, and that God is any way
served by my means."

But of course this could only go on for a time. Master Clitherow had allowed Margaret a free hand with
the bringing-up of the children, and he acquiesced in
Henry, the elder boy, being sent to a Catholic school in
France. That too was against the law, and the new council for Northern England sent for Master Clitherow.
Everyone knew that he was a Protestant — and so all his
wife's doings came to light. The court was careful not
to question John Clitherow too closely, but while he
was detained away from home, men were despatched to
search the house in Little Shambles. They found Margaret in the kitchen. But in the schoolroom were her two
children and a little foreign boy whom Margaret had
befriended. Their teacher saved himself by jumping out
of the window. The three children were left alone with
the disappointed and furious officers of the law. The

foreign boy gave way to their threats — he led them to the secret chapel and furnished them with the names of a number of men and women whom he knew to have taken part in the Masses said there.

One of them, Mistress Agnes Leech, was committed to York Castle, and Margaret was placed in the same cell, after undergoing a preliminary examination in which she infuriated the council.

The children, the servants, and poor John Clitherow himself, were divided among various prisons, and little Anne Clitherow, a child of ten, was exceedingly ill-treated for refusing to disclose anything of her mother's affairs, or to cease praying as her mother had taught her, or to attend a Protestant service.

Meanwhile Mistress Agnes and Mistress Margaret sat in their cell taking their supper of mouldy bread and water. They had no cups and they had no plates, had to manage as best they could without them. They did so; they laughed and joked at their own fancies and scandalized the jailers hugely by their ill-timed merriment. But before Margaret lay down to rest on the heap of verminous and rotten straw which was their bed, she knelt and thanked God fervently that no priest had been caught in the raid, and that none of her own children had been terrified into sinning. From Saturday to Monday the two women were left together. " Sister," said Margaret to Agnes, " we are so merry together that, unless we be parted, I fear me we shall come to lose the merit of our imprisonment."

(Mistress Leech was released on that occasion. Ten

years later she was again imprisoned and sentenced to be
burnt at the stake, for having persuaded an evangelical
minister to return to the Catholic Church. The sentence
of death was not carried out, but she was kept in prison
as long as Queen Elizabeth was alive.)

On the Monday Margaret was conducted to another
examination. On her way out of the prison she stopped
at a window from which she could look across the castle
yard at the imprisoned Catholics, thirty-five in number.
"Yet, before I go," she said, "I will make all my brethren and sisters on the other side of the hall merry." She
smiled and nodded, made a pair of gallows on her fingers and held them up.

Judge Clinch had the indictment read: Mistress
Clitherow was accused of having harboured priests,
heard Mass, and having sent her son to a Catholic school
abroad. "How say you, are you guilty of this indictment
or not?"

"I know no offence whereof I should confess myself
guilty."

At this certain "lewd fellows" entered the hall, carrying chalices, vestments and books. They put on the vestments, made unseemly fun with the vessels and traves-
tied the Mass. Some of the public in the galleries
laughed and encouraged them to go on. Margaret stood
very still with bent head and clasped hands.

Judge Clinch again implored her to submit to a trial
by a jury of her countrymen.

Margaret persisted in her refusal to plead. According
to the judicial procedure of the time this made a regular

hearing impossible. But she would not have the cause proceeded with. " Having made no offence, I need no trial. If you say I have offended, I will be tried by none but by God and your own conscience."

This was exactly what Judge Clinch did not want. If he could not save her, then let the jury condemn her to death, while he would be able to wash his hands of it. So he represented to her that, if she made it impossible for the jury to deal with her case, the law would compel him to deliver her over to the hardest of deaths — she would be pressed to death.

Margaret was steadfast in her refusal. A trial in due form would endanger others. Her husband and children and servants would then be called as witnesses. If they gave true evidence their memories would be charged ever after with having brought her to the gallows. If they lied, they would do injury to their own souls and offence to God. And she had an additional reason: if sentence were pronounced against her by a jury, it meant that many more men would be accomplices in her death than if she forced the council to take the sole responsibility.

She explained these reasons to the council, clearly, firmly and gently. Judge Clinch pronounced no sentence that day.

Like Pontius Pilate, Mr. Clinch was determined to do all he could to save the prisoner, short of running any personal risk. And at the next examination he tried to lure her on, reminding her that the only witness against her was a little boy.

" Indeed," said Mistress Clitherow, " I think you have no witnesses against me but children, which with an apple and a rod you may make to say what you will."

Now there occurred a pleasing incident. As the judge was about to pronounce sentence, a Puritan lay-preacher sprang to his feet. The Puritans were also in bad odour under Elizabeth, though at that time no one regarded them as of any particular political importance, so that as a rule they were treated with relative tolerance.

" My lord, take heed what you do. You sit here to do justice; this woman's case is touching life and death — you ought not, either by God's laws or man's, to judge her to die upon the slender witness of a boy; nor unless you have two or three sufficient men of very good credit to give evidence against her."

The judge said he might do so by the Queen's law.

" That may well be — but you cannot do it by God's law! "

Once more Judge Clinch tried to persuade the woman — if she would but refer her case to the laws of her country, some means of mercy might well be found.

But Margaret was inflexible. And the members of the council cried out: " Why stand we all the day about this naughty, wilful woman? Let us despatch her — "

Then Mr. Clinch pronounced judgment:

" — in the lowest part of the prison — you must be stripped naked, laid down, your back upon the ground . . . and be pressed to death, your hands and feet tied to posts, and a sharp stone under your back."

Margaret Clitherow answered: " If this judgment be

according to your own conscience, I pray God send you
better judgment before Him."

She was sent back to prison. When the turnkey looked
into her cell in the evening she sat singing. She only
asked for news of her husband and children — on being
told that no one intended them any harm she at once
appeared as cheerful and happy as was her wont.

Then came visitors — only those whom the council
sent to her. They all strove to shake her firmness — some
with harsh words, others with kindness. First came a
succession of Protestant clergymen, who talked to her
by the hour. One of them asked her: " *Then what is the
Church?* "

Margaret answered: " It is that wherein the true Word
of God is preached, which Christ left to His Apostles,
and to their successors ministering the Seven Sacraments,
which the same Church hath always observed, the Doctors preached, and Martyrs and Confessors witnessed.
This is the Church I believe to be true."

Calmly and in plain words the young woman con-
fessed her willingness to die as a member of the Catholic
Church: " My cause is God's, and it is a great comfort
for me to die in His quarrel: flesh is frail, but I trust in
my Lord Jesu, that He will give me strength to bear
all troubles and torments which shall be laid upon me
for His sake."

On the third day came the brave Puritan — Wiggington — who had spoken in court. He preached to her for
several hours, and with unshakable composure Margaret

199

explained to him what the Church really teaches about
sin and salvation, God's grace and the works of men —
she even tried by simple explanations to correct his false
ideas about indulgences and the significance of images.
But she must have been tired — after so many days' separation from her husband and children, and with death
before her eyes.

As a good Protestant Wiggington asked her whether
she possessed assurance of salvation. As a good Catholic
Margaret Clitherow answered: " I am yet living — but
if I persevere to the end, I verily believe I shall be
saved."

Her father-in-law came; he was mayor of York that
year. He promised to get her pardoned if only she would
yield a little: " do therefore something, and you shall
have mercy." He tempted, flattered, threatened, implored his daughter-in-law — at last he threw himself on
his knees before her. His visit was the most painful to
Margaret. They had always been very fond of each
other. But she bore it and stood firm.

Then came another clergyman. This one spoke kindly
to her. Margaret begged him to say no more:

" I ground my faith upon Jesu Christ, and by Him I
steadfastly believe to be saved, as is taught in the Catholic Church through all Christendom, and promised to remain with her unto the world's end, and hell gates shall
not prevail against it: and by God's assistance I mean to
live and die in the same faith; for if an angel come from
heaven, and preach any other doctrine than we have received, the Apostle biddeth us not to believe him.

Therefore, if I should follow your doctrine, I should disobey the Apostle's commandment."

The eve of Lady Day, Friday, March 25, 1586, was Margaret's last night upon earth. She had asked to have someone with her: "not for any fear of death, for it is my comfort; but the flesh is frail — ."

So they sent her a Protestant woman who was in prison for debt. She was a kind person, but what was she to do — ? Margaret Clitherow knelt on the stone floor and prayed in mortal anguish, and the other, Mistress Yoward, looked at her a while and pitied her sorely — but then she grew sleepy and had to lie down, and so she fell asleep. About midnight she woke up — Margaret was still kneeling on the same spot, but now she was no longer afraid — there was a radiant calm in her face. It was not so much that she looked happy, but rather as if she already experienced that of which all human happiness is a reflection. Mistress Yoward lay still, gazing at her companion, and had no thought of falling asleep again. It was about three in the morning when at last she saw Margaret rise and come to the fireside. The stones perhaps retained a trace of warmth — Margaret lay down and fell asleep at once.

When she awoke about six she was in her customary cheerful humour. And then she proposed to Mistress Yoward: "Stay with me and see me die." As anyone might say to a friend: "Come and see me off, won't you?" But Mistress Yoward had not the slightest desire to do so; she thought it horrible that so young and sweet

2 0 1

and pretty a woman was to die. But she offered to speak to some of her friends — she would get them to throw heavier weights upon Margaret, so that the end might come more quickly. Margaret said she must not do that: " God defend that I should procure any to be guilty of my death and blood."

At eight o'clock they came and fetched her. She sent her hat with a last greeting to her husband, in sign that she had always loved him above all in the world, after her God and Saviour. To her little daughter she sent her hose and shoes.

Then she set out barefoot on her last journey. From the condemned cell by Old Ouse Bridge to the Toll-booth, the old stone house on the other side of the river, was no long way. A crowd of people watched her go — they saw that she was smiling. And when Margaret was aware of all these faces with their look of sorrow and terror, she called out to comfort them: " This is as short a way to heaven as any other." She carried over her arm a long white garment; her shroud, which she had made in prison.

On reaching the vaulted cellar she knelt down. In front of her she had a heavy oaken door, the weights, the executioner and his assistants — enough to meditate upon, if she wished.

One of the Protestant ministers came forward and offered to pray with her. Margaret answered in a firm voice: " I will not pray with you, and you shall not pray with me; neither will I say Amen to your prayers, nor shall you to mine."

Does anyone think it could be easy for her to meet death, cut off in her inmost soul from all human intercourse? The gentle, sociable Mistress Clitherow had never made any distinction between co-religionists and heretics, when there was an opportunity of helping anyone in any way. And she had said time after time that she forgave everyone, she wished well to all. There was a spirit and a set of ideas with which she would not ally herself, even ostensibly, in death as in life.

She prayed on her knees for the Church, for the Pope, for all spiritual pastors, and then for all temporal sovereigns. Here she was interrupted — she must not pray for Queen Elizabeth in such company. Margaret continued undisturbed: " — and especially for Elizabeth, Queen of England, that God turn her to the Catholic faith, and that after this mortal life she may receive the blessed joy of heaven. For I wish as much good to her Majesty's soul as to mine own."

She was urged to confess that she suffered death for treason. In as loud and clear a voice as before Margaret answered: " No. I die for the love of my Lord Jesu."

Then the sheriff bade her undress: " For you must die naked, as judgment was given and pronounced against you."

For an instant it seemed that Margaret's courage failed. She was an honest man's wife, the mother of three children — and she threw herself on her knees, begging to be spared this. It was in vain. Then she asked that some women might be admitted, to stand about her as she undressed. This was granted; the men turned their backs meanwhile, and she was allowed to put on her shroud.

After that she lay down calmly on the earthen floor, clasped her hands below her chin, and the executioners placed the sharp stone under her back and the door over her. But the sheriff said her hands must be tied to the posts.

Obediently she stretched out her clasped hands from below the door, the executioners parted them and bound them fast. She now lay in the position of the Body on a crucifix.

The assistants threw the heavy weights upon the door. Those who stood around heard the crack of breaking bones, and blood began to ooze from under the door. And a faint voice moaned: " Jesu! Jesu! Jesu! have mercy upon me! — dear Jesu! I suffer this for Thee — "

Beside himself with repugnance the sheriff shouted for more weights — " come on with some stones — "

But it went on and on. The women who had been led out of the room could hear that it was not yet over. They pressed against the door, crying out wildly that the men must make an end of it at once. And still the piteous little voice was heard moaning: " Jesu — Jesu — "

At last, after more than a quarter of an hour, she died.

The body was allowed to lie there until three o'clock. In this connection Margaret's biographers remind us that three o'clock on Friday is an hour that arouses certain memories in Christians. — The body was then taken outside the city wall and buried in a rubbish-heap. Six weeks later some Catholics disinterred it and carried it away — no one knows whither. But one hand had been severed from the body. A delicately shaped little hand, brown and withered, clenched in the agony of death — this is the relic of Margaret Clitherow which the Catholics of England venerate to-day. It is in St. Mary's Convent, York.

This happened, then, on a Friday. Nobody told the two imprisoned children that their mother was dead. On the contrary, little Anne was told by some Protestants that if she would not go to their church and hear a Protestant sermon, her mother would be put to death. So the child went, to save her mother's life.

Then we hear no more of Margaret Clitherow's children for some years.

John Clitherow was completely crushed by sorrow and horror at his wife's fate. He had not even been allowed to bid her farewell — he had only received her last greeting, with her hat.

Some time after he married again, a Protestant woman this time. It is natural enough that he had had his fill of tragedy and therefore chose as his second wife one with whom he could be sure he was running no such risk. We have no means of knowing whether he consoled himself, or whether he ever forgot Margaret. But it is sadly probable that Master Clitherow had no eye for the true consolation — he can hardly have seen that Margaret had run the race to the end and won the precious garland. And perhaps it would be unreasonable to expect it of him. In other ways he prospered; in course of time he filled various honourable positions in the corporation of York.

Then we hear again, after a lapse of some years, of Anne Clitherow being imprisoned at Lancaster on account of her religion. Her father secured her release on condition of her being handed over to the instruction of " learned and pious preachers." Evidently they were not very successful — perhaps Anne's confidence in such people had received its death-blow in her childhood. In any case she was at Louvain three years later — whether she had been banished or had fled from England. Her age was now about thirty-three. Anne Clitherow took the veil in St. Ursula's Convent at Louvain; many other exiled English girls were already among the nuns there.

How it was that Margaret's younger boy managed to escape to France I do not know. But both Henry Clitherow and his brother became priests.

So for the mother and for the three children who had been through such bitter and cruel sufferings the story ends as a real Christmas tale ought to end.

TO ST. JAMES

PROPOSAL FOR A NEW PRAYER

 Perhaps you will say we have prayers enough? It may be so — if we only made such serious practice of them as our holy Church teaches us, we should not require any more. In my own case, unfortunately, I must confess that a little extra prayer such as I am going to propose would be very useful. If the clergy think there is need of it, they will be kind enough to put it into shape — and perhaps in time we might develop into a Society of St. James, or whatever it ought to be called. But here is the proposal:

That once daily we should pray:

"Set a watch, O Lord, before my mouth, and a door of prudence around my lips; that my heart incline not to evil words to make excuses in sins.[1]

Our Father. Hail Mary.

Saint James, pray for us.

Saint Peter Martyr, pray for us."

(Do you remember Fra Angelico's picture of St. Peter Martyr with his finger on his lips?)

[1] From the liturgy of the Mass: the Priest's prayer at incensing the Altar.

Perhaps we might include St. Philip Neri — but, as I said, the clergy will have to take it in hand and give the prayer a proper form. I am only suggesting.

The object of course will be to seek supernatural grace to enable us to take better care of our tongues than most of us are in the habit of doing. So that we may get out of the way of talking so much about our neighbours, may refrain from passing on everything we know for certain and a great deal of which we know nothing at all for certain, may be content to see a rumour fly past our door without asking it to come in so that we too may have a look at it.

"Nugigeri gesta mulier dimergit honesta.
        Ee druckner sqwaller fore goodh koness dör," [1]

as Peder Laale says. And we may be sure he was not the first to say it; the proverb must be much older.[2]

Do you know a book called "The Ancren Riwle" — the Rule of recluses? It was written by an old English Bishop for three damsels of high birth, sisters, who had bidden the world farewell and built themselves a little "anchorhold" — somewhere about the year 1200. They had not embraced any of the existing Rules, and the Bishop writes that if any person ask them to what Order they belong, they are to answer: "the Order of St. James, who was God's Apostle, and for his great holiness was called God's brother."

[1] Slander ever drowns before a good woman's door.
[2] Peder Laale (late 15th century) is famous for his collection of proverbs in (dog) Latin and Danish. — (Tr.)

In that section of the book which the worthy Father entitles " On keeping the heart" he explains to the young women the Rule of St. James with regard to " hearing." (They had already debarred themselves from the temptation of running about and chatting.) The old gentleman is plain-spoken — there is no mistake about his realism when giving advice about the affairs of this world. On account of that section of his Rule which deals with spiritual life he has sometimes been called the father of English mysticism. But he is no mystic when speaking " of hearing ":

" Against all evil speech, my dear sisters, stop your ears, and have a loathing of the mouth that vomiteth out poison. Evil speech is threefold — poisonous, foul, idle: idle speech is evil; foul speech is worse; poisonous speech is the worst. All that from which no good cometh is idle and needless; ' And of such speech,' saith our Lord, ' shall every word be reckoned and account given,' why the one spoke it and the other listened to it. And yet, this is the least of the three evils. What! How, then, shall men give account of the three evils, and especially of the worst? What! How of the worst? that is, of poisonous and of foul speech; not only they who speak it, but they who listen to it. Foul speech is of lechery and of other uncleanness, which unwashen mouths speak at times. Men should stop the mouth of him who spitteth out such filth in the ears of any recluse, not with sharp words, but with hard fists.

" Poisonous speech is heresy, and direct falsehood, backbiting, and flattery. These are the worst. Heresy,

God be thanked, prevaileth not in England; but lying is so evil a thing that St. Austin saith 'That thou shouldest not tell a lie to shield thy father from death.' God himself saith that he is truth; and what is more against truth than is lying and falsehood? 'The devil,' we are told, 'is a liar, and the father of lies.' She, then, who moveth her tongue in lying, maketh of her tongue a cradle to the devil's child, and rocketh it diligently as nurse.

"Backbiting and flattery, and instigating to do any evil, are not fit for man to speak; but they are the devil's blast and his own voice. If these ought to be far from all secular men — what! how ought recluses to hate and shun them, that they may not hear them? Hear them, I say, for she who speaketh with them is no recluse at all. 'The serpent,' saith Solomon, 'stingeth quite silently; and she who speaketh behind another what she would not before is not a whit better.' Hearest thou how Solomon eveneth a backbiter to a stinging serpent? Such she certainly is. She is of serpents' kindred, and she who speaketh evil behind another beareth poison in her tongue. The flatterer blinds a man, and puts a prickle in the eyes of him whom he flattereth. The backbiter often cheweth man's flesh on Friday, and pecketh with his black bill living carcases; as he that is the devil's raven of hell; yet, if he would tear in pieces and pluck with his bill, rotten stinking flesh, as raven's nature is; that is, if he would not speak evil against any but those who are corrupt and stink in the filth of their sins, it were yet the less sin: but he lighteth upon living flesh; teareth and dismembereth it; that is, he slandereth such as are alive in God. He is too greedy a raven, and too bold withal.

" On the other hand, observe now, of what kind are the two offices in which these two jugglers serve their lord, the devil of hell. It is a foul thing to speak of, but fouler to be it, and it is always so. They are the devil's dirt-men, and wait continually in his privy. The office of the flatterer is to cover and to conceal the hole of the privy; and this he doth as oft as he with his flattery and with his praise concealeth and covereth from man his sin; for nothing stinketh fouler than sin, and he concealeth and covereth it, so that he doth not smell it. The backbiter discloseth and uncovereth it, and so openeth that filth that it stinketh widely. Thus, they are busy in this foul employment, and strive with each other about it. Such men stink of their stinking trade, and make every place stink that they come to. May our Lord shield you, that the breath of their stinking throat may never come nigh you. Other speech polluteth and defileth; but this poisoneth the heart and the ears both. That you may know them the better, listen to their marks.

" There are three kinds of flatterers. The first are bad enough; yet the second are worse; but the third are worst of all. The first, if a man is good, praiseth him in his presence, and, without scruple, maketh him still better than he is; and, if he saith or doth well, he extolleth it too highly with excessive praise and commendation. The second, if a man is depraved and sins so much in word and deed, that his sin is so open that he may nowise wholly deny it, yet he, the flatterer, in the man's own presence extenuates his guilt. 'It is not, now,' saith he, 'so exceeding bad as it is represented. Thou art not, in this matter, the first, nor wilt thou be the last. Thou hast many fellows. Let it be, my good man. Thou goest not alone. Many do much worse.'

"The third flatterer cometh after, and is the worse, as I said before, for he praiseth the wicked and his evil deeds; as he who said to the knight who robbed his poor vassals, 'Ah, sir! truly thou doest well. For men ought always to pluck and pillage the churl; for he is like the willow, which sprouteth out the better that it is often cropped.' Thus doth the false flatterer blind those who listen to him, as I said before, and covereth their filth so that it may not stink: and that is a great calamity. For, if it stunk, he would be disgusted with it, and so run to confession, and there vomit it out, and shun it thereafter.

"Backbiters, who bite other men behind, are of two sorts: but the latter sort is the worse. The former cometh quite openly, and speaketh evil of another, and speweth out his venom, as much as ever comes to his mouth, and throweth out, at once, all that the poisonous heart sends up to the tongue. But the latter proceedeth in a quite different manner, and is a worse enemy than the other; yet, under the cloak of a friend. He casteth down his head, and begins to sigh before he says anything, and makes sad cheer, and moralizes long without coming to the point, that he may be the better believed. But, when it all comes forth, then it is yellow poison. 'Alas and alas! ' he saith, ' wo is me, that he or she hath got such a reputation. Enough did I try, but it availed me nothing, to effect an amendment here. It is long since I knew of it, but yet it should never have been exposed by me; but now it is so widely published by others that I cannot gainsay it. Evil they call it, and yet it is worse. Grieved and sorry I am that I must say it; but indeed it is so; and that is much sorrow. For many other things, he, or she, is truly to be commended, but not for this, and grieved I am for it. No man can defend them.' These are the devil's serpents which Solomon speaketh of. May our Lord, by his grace, keep away your ears from their venomous tongues, and never permit you to smell that foul pit which they uncover, like as the flatterers cover and hide it, as I said before. Let those whom it behoveth uncover it to themselves and hide it from others. That is an essential service, and not to those only who would hate that filth as soon as they should smell it.

" Now, my dear sisters, keep your ears far from all evil speaking, which is thus threefold, idle, foul, and venomous. People say of anchoresses that almost every one hath an old woman to feed her ears; a prating gossip who tells her all the tales of the land; a magpie that chatters to her of every thing that she sees or hears; so that it is a common saying, ' From miln and from market, from smithy and from nunnery, men bring tidings.' Christ knows, this is a sad tale; that a nunnery, which should be the most solitary place of all, should be evened to those very three places in which there is the most idle discourse. But would to God, dear sisters, that all the others were as free as ye are of such folly." [1]

Well, these were a few little reflections taken from everyday life about the year of Our Lord 1200. Are they entirely out of date in our time, I wonder?

Here is a little story which is a good deal more recent — from the time when I was a girl — round about 1900. I was on a visit to my grandfather in Denmark, and one fine summer morning my aunt and I walked out to call on good old " Sister Jörgensen " who lived some way off in the country. (Aunt was a Methodist, so all her friends were Sister This or Brother That. And they were all such nice people, and like good Christians they strove to keep Our Lord's ten commandments, and it was not till they came to the eighth that they showed any sign of fatigue. But at the eighth they seemed unable to take any more fences on the road to heaven; they were apt to give themselves a long rest there.)

We found " Sister Jörgensen " very much upset, and as soon as we were seated at her luncheon table — it was a beautiful dream of a Danish luncheon table, by the way — and had swallowed our first cup of coffee, she opened her heart to us. " Now isn't it shocking the way folks gossip? Just listen to this, Sister Gyth — the other day I was down in my garden picking raspberries and one of the men from Enggaard comes riding along the

[1] This extract from the *Ancren Riwle* is here given in the modernized version by the Rev. James Morton, which was first printed by the Camden Society in 1856 and is now available under the title of *The Nun's Rule* in The Medieval Library (London: Chatto & Windus. St. Louis: B. Herder) . — (Tr.)

road, and he says to me he's going to fetch the doctor to the housekeeper, she'd been kicked to death pretty near —and I thought he said, by Cohen. So says I, oh, but how terrible—I says, when I was down at the shop, isn't it terrible, the steward at Enggaard's kicked his housekeeper so bad they've had to fetch the doctor to her—.

"But what do you think the next thing was? Yesterday Herr Cohen comes in here as angry as you please and threatens to have the law of me, for saying he'd kicked his housekeeper so she had to take to her bed—it was a *cow* that kicked her, when she went to fetch something from the cow-shed.[1] But isn't it awful to think anyone could be so ill-natured as to go straight to the steward and tell him I'd been saying he'd kicked his housekeeper? I can't imagine what harm I'd ever done them. But isn't it shocking the way folks gossip about you? "

Such in effect was the tale of Sister Jörgensen.

It is the fashion at present to talk at random about the Nordic race and its qualities and characteristics. I do not know whether a propensity for gossiping is a racial peculiarity among the fair Nordic folk, but certain it is that all the institutions and inventions which have for their object the promotion and nurturing of gossip have originated within this group of peoples— coffee parties and five o'clock teas and " Kaffeekränchen " and sewing bees and mothers' meetings, illustrated weeklies, the American art of interviewing and all the rest of it—not forgetting clubs. I don't know

[1] This requires a word of explanation: " the cow " in Danish is *Koen*, which sounds exactly like the steward's name, Cohen. — (Tr.)

whether this mania for discussing other people's affairs is more strongly innate in us than in the Latin peoples, for instance. (The Celts do not gossip, so people say who have lived among them; they always invent their stories out of hand.) Or is it that the Church has always kept an eye on the eighth commandment and people's attitude towards a matter which seems to leave their consciences so strangely unaffected? I have the impression that in Catholic countries gossip exists more as a weed growing wild — to be sure, people gossip there too, but as far as I have seen very little is done to cultivate gossip as a garden or indoor plant.

The Reformation of course has played its part. It took gossip into its service, actually consecrated a certain type of gossip for religious use. Let us just imagine, for instance, what a quantity of slander was required to induce the people calmly to acquiesce in the suppression of the monasteries and the conversion of their estates — a great part of which had been given and was used for the aid of the necessitous among themselves, living and dead — into private or Crown property. Or to accustom them to accept it as reasonable that their parish priest should have a legitimate family which was bound to be his first care. Or think of the systematic perversion of domestic religious tradition which was required before the whole nation could be made homeless in its own spiritual history. And although we Catholics have abundant and daily opportunities of observing the decay of other articles of the Reformation's heritage — such as reliance on the Holy Scriptures, or a sense of the value

of a concrete creed — yet in one point all the sects that
derive from the Reformation and all their offshoots
seem faithful to the family tradition — in their appre-
ciation of the value of slander in religious life, and in
ecclesiastical history.

Now most of us Catholics in Sweden, Norway and
Denmark are converts or the children of converts; we
form a tiny minority among a people of coffee parties,
weekly papers, societies and meetings. All I suggest is
that next time we prepare ourselves for confession, we
should take up the eighth commandment and give as
much attention to seeing how we stand towards it as we
do to the rest of our preparation. For instance: how did
we behave the last time we were invited out — or the
last time we gave a party? Let us take the catechism and
study it, see what it has to say on this subject. There
are in particular some little subsidiary clauses behind
an " or " — " or magnify our neighbour's real faults."
" Or unnecessarily reveal his hidden faults." And something about unfounded suspicion and presumptuous
judgment.

And then we ought to read the good old Epistle of
St. James. As you know, what he says about the tongue
is in the third chapter. But if one has time, the whole
epistle may well be studied, from beginning to end.
Luther did not like St. James. But perhaps the feeling
would have been mutual, if the two Doctors had met
here on earth.

I do not mean that we, members of the prospective
sisterhood (and fraternity!) of St. James, ought literally

to start up as though bitten by the above-mentioned serpent whenever anybody begins: " Have you heard about Mrs. So-and-So? " crossing ourselves like semaphores and snatching at a book or a rosary to scare away the serpent. But there is one thing we must remember: we have all grown up in a state of society in which everyone more or less has a passion for chatting about other people's intimate affairs; in which unfortunately a rumour generally manages to keep afloat a very long time before it reaches the door of the good woman, where according to the proverb it ought to sink to the bottom. And don't you know the type of person who — innocently, I was going to say, if it were not just the opposite — considers it a mark of intelligence to be suspicious and a mark of naïvety to insist that one ought to believe the best, until one has certain evidence of anything worse? A state of society which makes a parlour game of climbing over the eighth commandment, like children jumping over a fence and back again.

This does not mean that we are to condemn ourselves to silence, like Trappists. But our aim should be rather to err on the side of renunciation than to insist on making full use of the freedom of speech allowed us by our religion. We in our part of the world are like people who have ruined their digestions by too much and too rich food, and we ought to diet ourselves for the rest of our lives; it takes so little to bring on an attack of our old malady — loquacity.

At a gathering at which Mme Elisabeth Leseur was

present the conversation turned upon a lady whose conduct had been such as to get her talked about.

" Why do you tell us this? " said Mme Leseur; " you know nothing about it; one can never be sure of rumours of this kind."

The lady addressed replied: " But it's quite certain — the affair is public property and proved over and over again."

" Very well," answered Mme Leseur, " in that case there is nothing more to be said about it."

I am sure you all know the story of St. Philip Neri and the hen. This is the version I have heard: St. Philip had among his penitents a woman who was an accomplished tale-bearer. One day she came to him again and had to confess that she had indulged in her besetting sin. St. Philip said: " Before I can give you absolution I impose this penance on you: that you go to the market and buy a hen — you can pluck it as you walk back; then come here and bring it to me."

The woman thought this an odd sort of penance, but she did as the holy man had ordered, came back and delivered the plucked hen at the confessional. " And now, my daughter, you are to go back the same way, collect all the down and feathers you have plucked from the hen and bring them to me." " But, Reverendo, that is impossible! " " My child, it is even more impossible for you to take back all the idle gossip and vain talk you have spread abroad, or to make good here on earth the transgressions of your sinful tongue."

So I think we ought to include St. Philip Neri as our third tutelary saint against gossip.

But in any case I propose that we begin with a prayer to St. James.

REPLY TO A PARISH PRIEST

(Extract from a private letter)

". . . but when, reverend father, you ask me: ' How does it come about that in these Essays,[1] which were written long before you became a Catholic, *marriage* is several times alluded to as a *Sacrament?* ' — this calls for a rather lengthy explanation. I shall therefore avail myself of your proposal and answer the question by a kind of open letter in the columns of *Credo.*"

[1] This refers to a former volume of *Etapper,* which has not been translated into English.

 I PREMISE a few observations: If any of the readers of *Credo* should be scandalized or shocked at what I am going to say, I beg them to remember that Our Lord caught me — as so many others like me — into His sheepfold straight out of the wilderness. Before we were received into the Catholic Church we had never known any kind of enclosure, even of the most provisory and unrestricted nature, which we could look upon as a fold we belonged to. We wandered like sheep upon the moors — but in any case it taught us something of how sheep fare when they relapse and become strays. It enables us to say something about how life appears to young people who quite consciously refuse to accept the Christian element in European civilization as anything but a human contribution. We know how people argue who look upon history merely as the results of men's growing insight into the laws of nature and into their own human nature — in short, as " evolution," to use the vague and indefinite popular term.

This is precisely the danger in all countries where Christianity is the tradition, but especially in those countries where some curtailed form of Christianity (protestant or reformed) has been favoured by the temporal power as a State Church; people are then very apt to imagine that this or that social institution or moral idea — which in reality has resulted from Europe having formerly accepted the dogmas of the Catholic Church — has arisen quite "naturally," in proportion as the nations "advanced" on their road from primitive barbarism to "higher civilization."

It is perhaps inevitable that in countries where the clergy form part of State officialdom and the priests are Government servants, both clergy and congregation should be disposed to identify Christian with civil morality. The mediæval Church strove to make States conform in their legislation to the commandments of Christianity. But the mediæval Church had a long and manifold experience of the impossibility of ever stabilizing such conformity. Against the commandment of Christianity to seek *first* the kingdom of God, human nature will always assert its right to seek *first* its own. And every single group of men which obtains control of society and is able to enforce its views in the fashioning of laws, will know how to maintain its special interests. (These need not always, or indeed primarily, be what is called "material interests." They may just as well be the ideals of a single man or a single class, to which they are willing to sacrifice life and welfare.)

The Church knew this. St. Paul had his own experiences in this matter, as appears from his epistles. And from century to century the Church had had occasion to learn that even her own consecrated servants were prone to fail her here. She had continually to endure Gethsemane nights, when Judas betrayed, and the other disciples sought their own safety. New saints and new reformers had continually to rebuild what their brethren had ruined. Nevertheless, at the time when the " Reformation " broke out, the Church had succeeded in instilling into the consciousness of Christendom a kind of latent demand that the doctrines of Christianity should be taken as the pattern of life, and that the temporal power should in some way or other help and support people who wished to live as Christians — should make an end of conditions and institutions which were a downright temptation to breaches of Christianity, and legislate in such a way that in abiding by the laws of their country the people would also be practising Christianity.

This in reality is the triumph of the Catholic Church. In spite of all her weaknesses the mediæval Church had won this moral victory over the pagan propensities of princes and peoples, over the egoisms and idiosyncrasies of classes and individuals. In spite of the diversity of language and temperament, in spite of the changing frontiers and conflicting interests of kingdoms and principalities, their mutual antipathies determined by linguistic differences and national psychology, Europe had really become a unity, " Christendom." There was a unity of *faith* — a prevailing conviction that what the

Church taught was the Truth itself concerning the origin, object and meaning of human life — no matter how the individual in his private life attempted to escape the consequences of such a belief, or at any rate to get out of them as cheaply and easily as he could. But if it had not been the general *conviction* that the Church taught objective truth in teaching that Jesus Christ is very God, born of the incomprehensible God the Father from all eternity, and at the same time truly man born of the Virgin Mary, that the Bible is His word — if this purely intellectual conviction of the truth of Christianity had not been as firmly rooted in the peoples as the individual's willingness to take the consequences of his faith was weak and wavering — then it is clear that not even the most simple-minded of fanatics could have imagined that Christianity would be able to hold its own as a State religion. That it could be left to kings, princes or to any organ of popular self-government to direct the religious life of the nations, and that the State religion could nevertheless continue to be Christianity — this proves more than anything else to what extent the Church had succeeded in the first fifteen hundred years of her life in fulfilling her mission — that of preaching the Gospel to the nations in such a way that they believed in it.

And in reality the nations have lived on the aftereffects of this mediæval conviction of the self-evident character of Christian truth, long after the roots of the faith had been severed, one by one. Ideas, whose only origin is one or other of the Catholic dogmas, were still regarded as obviously true, long after the dogma on which they rested had been forgotten or contested or rejected — because the acceptance of the Catholic doctrine in the past had left such deep traces in tradition and habits of thought that ordinary people assumed it to be " natural " to think thus.

I will illustrate what I mean by a single example:

In ordinary respectable circles there is still quite a common feeling that there is something peculiarly sinister and disgraceful about suicide. People who regard appearances still try to conceal the fact if any member of their family has taken his own life. It is assumed with full justification that a person must be quite uncannily outside the tradition of ordinary decent people if he can say: " My father shot himself," or " My sister took her life with veronal," without showing any emotion essentially different from that with which he might announce: " My father died of cancer," " My sister died in a tuberculosis sanatorium."

Yet it is only on the basis of the whole and uncurtailed doctrine of the Christian Church that suicide becomes absolutely iniquitous. If one accepts Christianity as the very truth, it is a hideous and terrible sin for a person who is fully accountable to take his life because he will not hold out and wait till God opens the door of death — refuses to bear a suffering, submit to a humiliation, while God wills that he is to endure life upon earth.

But what about a person who does not believe in any personal God, or at any rate in a God who directly cares for every single one of His creatures, holds His hand over every human being just as much when that being is so benumbed by sickness and pain, so crushed by the blows of fate, that he is quite unconscious of the protecting hand — ?

Why yes, suicide is cowardly, choruses the man in the street, who knows it to be an old tradition that suicide is a disgrace, though he has no clear, dogmatically defined belief in God's detailed interest in human destinies nor in its being a sin against a personal God to yield to every impulse of self. In following his own impulses he is in the habit of saying, he believes that God is good and God understands him better than men. Perhaps he will plead that Jesus was full of understanding, since he has always heard this said. He has not grasped that the Jesus of the Gospels *understands* men in the sense that He *sees through* them, knows all about them, all that they would wish to deny both to God and to themselves. But an ordinary modern person uses the term " understand " in quite another sense: he who " understands " me is the one who takes at its face value all I tell him about myself and admits all the excuses I can invent for this or that action I have committed. And it is really comic — besides being tragic — that the greater the efforts that are made to enable everybody to read the Bible for himself or at least to think he knows what is in that book, the more wide-spread is the idea that God's supernatural wisdom consists in His accepting all the excuses we offer, even though no man on earth would accept them.

So we see that an ordinary average person, who still has some points on which he is not influenced by the currents of thought of our time, continues to say that suicide is a disgrace because it is cowardly to take one's own life. Perhaps he himself would never be able to summon up the brutal *physical* courage needed in order to put a revolver into one's mouth and pull the trigger, or jump over the side of a steamer at night. No doubt it always requires a certain measure of physical courage for a sound and healthy person to destroy himself. (If the suicide is a physical wreck it is another matter.) It is true that many people are driven to suicide by miserable moral cowardice: a little loose-living till-thief sneaks out of this world like a man who cheats a hotel, living like a prince at the expense of the proprietor and vanishing before the bill is presented. A speculator ruins people wholesale, driving families out of house and home and wrecking the plans of parents for their children's future — and then blows out his brains to avoid the reckoning and the just indignation of his victims.

But imagine a person who is ignorant of religion and self-taught in morals. On the basis of traditional opinions which he has absorbed unconsciously, without analysing them in their origin, and of ideals which accord with his natural tendencies, he has formed his own conceptions of right and wrong, of honest or dishonest living. He feels in himself the normal, human instinct of self-development, of living in a way that seems to him humanly worthy. Then he yields to the temptation of doing what is easy, instead of what is right — the eternal human temptation to be false to something which

2 3 1

non-Christians also feel within them and which they call their better self. He picks himself up, once, many times, and falls again and is false to his own ideals. It was the experience of the saints — St. Teresa and St. Aloysius, for instance — that our own nature has a terrible inclination to droop, to catch at cheap and handy satisfactions which we know in our hearts to be incapable of satisfying us, to shirk (just for once) making an effort — to be lazy and slack and cold, coarsened and stagnant. Our man has never understood the dogma of original sin, or he has taken the story of the Fall to be a Jewish parable — at the worst he is infected with some Rousseauish ideas about the fundamental goodness of human nature, and discovers that in any case his own is not good; so he supposes he must be an inferior person, an odious moral deficient, a weaker character than the normal human being (or a special victim of fate!). He does not believe in God's saving grace nor in means of grace which may give him strength to fight on, hope of victory. So he judges himself unworthy to live — chooses to execute himself with his own hand while he has a little courage and honour left in him. Is this cowardice?

Or a person is hopelessly ill — knows that the issue is certain and he must die. But before the end comes he may be faced with years of helplessness, hebetude, idiocy. Humanly speaking he himself will be useless and loathsome, his illness will entail expense on others, it will be troublesome to nurse him, those dear to him will be pained by the sight of his sufferings. Better to relieve them of such a burden as he is bound to become. It is no part of *his* belief that God saved the world by dying on a cross; St. Paul's words about " filling up in his flesh those things that are wanting of the sufferings of Christ " are meaningless to him. That he may accomplish something merely by suffering, that the burdens and sufferings he will impose on others have a significance in God's dispensation, he *cannot* believe (and I admit it must be exceedingly difficult to believe that the troubles we impose on others against our will can serve a good purpose) . Is it cowardice for a sick person like this to cut short his life?

I willingly admit, therefore, that in confessing I have no doubt that suicide is a sin, I am following the doctrine of the Catholic Church, not my own conscience. Because I believe that the dogmas of the Catholic Church contain absolute truths, I can learn to *understand* why suicide must be sin — when committed by a person who has the full use of his intelligence and has been instructed of the mystery of the Cross, it is the absolute sin which cannot be atoned for, since the suicide himself puts an end to the time of grace. But if I were merely to follow my own conscience and my natural uninstructed intelligence, I should say of course that suicide *may* be a scurvy way of sneaking off and leaving others to pay one's bills. But it *may* also be a heroic action, and so the pagans in all ages have regarded the matter. And unless I am mistaken the Catholic Church too has always held that even if an act is material sin — that is, even if he who commits it believes, for want of proper instruction, that it is a good or a justifiable act — it only becomes formal sin, for which the sinner can be made answerable, when he is sufficiently instructed to know he is doing wrong. We may none the less admire Hannibal and Mithridates, who would not survive the defeat of their nation. The classical statue of a Gallic warrior who has killed his wife and still supports her body with one hand while the other aims the dagger at his breast, is expressive of heroism also to us (the archæologists, by the way, now seem to think it represents something else, and it has been wrongly restored, but that is of no consequence in this connection). The point is that the Gaul acts rightly according to his own principles in killing his wife and himself in order to escape slavery. He has never seen a crucifix and does not know what is meant by God ruling from the Tree; he has never heard of the slave Blandina in the arena of Lyons or of the slave Felicitas of Carthage. He can know nothing of the faith which makes bondwomen freer and more princely than heathen queens.

Meanwhile it has gradually become the custom for Protestant churches to bury suicides exactly as though no disagreement existed between them and the church. Just as it has gradually become the practice, at any rate in Norway, on the death of a celebrated person, for the church to open its doors wide for his body and give it a great funeral, even if the deceased has declared all his life that he had no sympathy with the same church and believed very little of what it taught.

But all that can be said in defence of a suicide, or of

a declared freethinker, and that on which his Christian relatives may base their hopes for the dead man's soul, is that he actually stood outside the Christian Church, perhaps through no fault of his own, or the fault may not have been entirely his. The material sins he committed were committed in good faith, in his own eyes they were right and defensible acts. And He who is to judge of *that* is all-knowing and is mercy and justice itself.

In the Middle Ages the suicide and the notorious sinner who died without having received the Sacraments — the visible signs whereby invisible grace is imparted — were often buried at high-water mark, "where sea and green sward meet." As one of the sagas of St. Gudmund tells us, the age had some sort of notion of the circulation of the waters. And included in this circulation are the waters of Jordan which had washed Our Saviour's body, when He entered the river to be baptized by St. John. So all the water on earth is sanctified thereby and becomes the symbol of the grace whose limits no man dare define.

But a Church must abide by men's notification — in signs and words and deeds — whether they wish to be within it or outside it. It must excommunicate those who openly declare that they do not believe what it preaches and will not accept God's grace, in any case not by those means which it is the duty of the Church to administer. It cannot cast out a sinner who continues to assert that he believes what the Church teaches — even if he does not live according to his faith — and demands

2 3 5

to be given the aid of its Sacraments in order to be able to live according to his faith in future. This has always appeared to me a clear and logical position — long before it occurred to me that the Catholic Church really administered any such thing as positive grace. I have never been able to see anything presumptuous in her shutting people out and letting them in, according to the attitude they adopted towards her by an act of rebellion or of submission. In the last resort there is in every soul a substratum of ultimate secrets which are known to no one but God — however conscientiously the soul may have tried to represent itself as it is to its rightful confessor. This then is precisely the moral of all the mediæval legends — of dead men who have passed away fortified by all the rites of the Church, and nevertheless return one fine day, or night, and harrow their spiritual pastor and their sorrowing relatives with the most gruesome revelations concerning their present condition — of Hosts that fly out of the priest's hand straight into the mouth of a poor penitent who has been relegated to the lower end of the church — of monks who have died without receiving absolution for a sin and have been buried outside the cemetery of their brethren — and suddenly the dead man appears in choir or chapter-house, hand in hand with the Virgin Mary herself, who explains that there were extenuating or exculpating circumstances, known to God alone — .

On the other hand I do consider that the Protestant mode of proceeding was often presumptuous, when some clergyman or other took upon himself to declare that the dead man had really never meant what he had always said, or that what he had said was after all not his opinion — and that the deceased was all the same so excellent a fellow that the clergyman, going by his own ideas of God and of how Jesus ought really to be interpreted, felt justified in assuming something more or less definite about the relations between the deceased and God. — It seems to me presumptuous that anyone should claim such communion with a dead man, who while alive never acknowledged that any communion existed between himself and those who are burying him.

2

Now it is a fact that many of us began to be agnostics as soon as we began to go to school — for the result of all we learned was to make us doubt everything our elders wanted to have us believe. And many of us in any case gradually came to perceive that in finding it impossible to believe in Christianity we deprived of all rational meaning a mass of accepted social traditions and moral ideas — even if, purely as a matter of sentiment, it hurt us to be forced to say that these traditions were out of date. We saw, it is true, that people who had no more defined, dogmatic religious belief than ourselves considered that these moral ideas would continue to live, that tradition would be able to hold its own. For these ideas were the fruits of the sacred tree of "evolution," and even if they should evolve into something yet finer and "higher," this would be a kind of organic development, analogous to the growth of a tree or the growth of a human being from childhood to maturity.

One of these traditions, which is based wholly and solely on a Catholic dogma, is lifelong, monogamous *marriage*. Though, to be sure, it seemed to me and to many who shared my views that logically it must be a dogma common to all evangelical Christianity, that for Christians there could be no question of anything but lifelong, indissoluble monogamy as the only permissible form of marriage. But we were faced with the historical fact that all the founders of Protestant sects had agreed in throwing this dogma overboard. They had all accepted the view that in certain circumstances marriage may be dissolved and that divorced persons may marry again, even during the lifetime of their former partner. Luther had flirted freely with the idea of polygamy and permitted persons of rank at any rate to take a secondary wife. We were more or less acquainted with the historical development whereby the legal grounds of divorce had been multiplied — till the point was reached in our young days when all the various grounds of divorce were comprised in a single, fundamental pretext: it is sufficient ground for divorce if one of the parties desires it.

For that matter it was perhaps rather unfair of us to make such shocking fun of divorced people who insisted on starting a fresh connection with a church wedding, and of the unfortunate clergymen of the State church who undertook to dispense a " licence for adultery." But it is quite certain that, even if we had essentially other grounds for our total disbelief in the doctrines of the State church, one of the reasons for our being unable even to respect it was this: we thought it despicable, both intellectually and morally, for its members to divorce in defiance of the words of Christ in the Gospels, and yet claim to have a new connection sanctified in a Christian church. And we thought that the clergymen who performed such solemnizations, or accepted office in a State whose legislation on many points proceeded on un-Christian principles, were a pretty set of blackguards.

We could see nothing in marriage beyond a contract which was accepted by two persons and could be dissolved if one of the parties failed too glaringly in fulfilling it. But we realized that, if in some way or other God had a share in the contract, why then the case was entirely altered. But to us God was the great X — we did not even venture to assert that we disbelieved in His existence, or to have any opinion as to a life after this — we dared not even declare that we did *not* believe in God and a life after death, as did the orthodox freethinkers. Since roughly speaking all races of men had believed in something of the sort, this might well be an instinctive recognition of a reality. For all we knew, we might be no sooner dead and, as we hoped, done with it all, than we would be fated to start all over again. For, as we knew very well, there is no universal human belief that life after death is to be specially enjoyable or a thing to look forward to — on the contrary. In reality it is comparatively rare for primitive peoples to imagine the life hereafter as at all pleasant, so long as they have not been in contact with Christian missionaries. And the ideas of non-Christian civilized peoples regarding life after death are in general fairly pessimistic. (Islam arose on the very thresholds of Christianity, and this is characteristic.) There is certainly no danger that we former agnostics will forget that the Christian hope is a *virtue* — it is based on the promises of Jesus Christ and the belief that He was God and can keep what He has promised, and on nothing else. And, bad and stupid Catholics as we may be, we know at any rate why we pray: " Blessed be the fruit of thy womb, Jesus — who strengthens us in hope! "

In reality it did not require any prodigious experience of the world — no more than might be possessed by very youthful persons — to understand that, in asserting the only right form of marriage to be lifelong monogamy, without possibility of reprieve, even when relations between the partners become unhappy, the Church must have considered that the object of marriage was not primarily to assure the partners' welfare and happiness here on earth. The Church must intend that in some way marriage should primarily be subservient to the *eternal life* of mankind. So that after all it was not so extraordinarily difficult for us to see what the Catholic Church meant by her doctrine of the *Sacrament* of matrimony. —

It must be nearly twenty years ago that I received a

visit one evening from one of my friends. He had got
a divorce from his wife — openly and honestly, as one
said at that time; the fact was, he loved another, and
everybody implicated in the affair wished to be truth-
ful and loyal to everybody else. So his beloved had also
got a divorce from her husband, after the necessary
truth-telling, and then they had made an advance wedding trip and were now living apart, but just at this
time they were looking for a house, as in a month or
two they were to " bring their relations into order in
accordance with the laws of society." And now — just
as they were on the point of going off to inscribe themselves in the register as man and wife — my poor friend
had discovered that his beloved had been unfaithful to
him to such an extent that he was sore to his very soul
about it all. And this time she had postponed her truth-
telling, as she couldn't quite make up her mind which
of her lovers she loved best and would decide to go and
live with. She had simply fooled them both to the top
of their bent.

My friend was in despair, which was not to be won-
dered at, and he asked me from the bitterness of his
heart:

" Tell me, Sigrid, do you believe at all that a woman
can be true to a man? "

To which I made the decided answer: " No, I don't.
I not only believe but know that a woman can be true
till death, if she has an ideal which demands her fidelity. But true to a man — no, I don't believe any woman
can be that."

And to put it mildly it's an unreasonable thing to ask, I thought to myself, that a woman should be true to a man — seeing what men are. Or a man true to a woman, seeing what women are. But I probably had a feeling that it was rather a spirited thing to acknowledge this — and I meant every word of it. Among people who believed in nothing but purely human ideals — or ideal human beings — one was forced to acknowledge that men and women have never been faithful, unless their fidelity had an object superior to the individual.

For Catholics, of course, it needs no extraordinary courage to acknowledge this. Every Catholic who makes a moderately conscientious preparation for his confession, and in addition makes a practice of examining his conscience for two — or ten or five — minutes every day, must of course arrive at this result: if his (her) marriage were built upon no other foundation than mutual affection and respect, there would be nothing unreasonable in his (her) partner preferring, at any rate now and again, almost any other man (woman) of their circle of acquaintance. " Of all sinners I am the worst."

We did not fail to see that the Christian faith had brought with it all kinds of secondary and secular social advantages during the centuries in which Europe had professed Christianity. But I at any rate was aware that these had been as it were by-products which came about while the Church was pursuing her real aim — that of saving souls. I saw this because from childhood

I had been trained to look at history without allowing myself to be affected by the more or less libretto-like versions given by the summaries of school-books. I knew that the traditional European conception of marriage was thus a by-product of the Catholic dogma of the sacrament of marriage. It is certain that so long as people assume marriage to be monogamous and lifelong, there is a greater probability of happy marriages being not too rare and good homes not too few. Since in any case people have a strong encouragement to try to get the best out of their relationship when they know they cannot escape from it, and people rarely acquire any good thing without trying. And a great many people do not care to try anything in earnest, unless they know they are forced to.

But as a sacrament — a means of grace — marriage must have been instituted primarily to help people on the road to eternal salvation. On no other assumption is it at all likely that men could ever have claimed that it is, and must be, an indissoluble union, in which both parties in the first place undertake duties towards God, and towards each other *in God*. Even while the Church's doctrine of marriage was held to be objectively true and right practically all over Europe, adultery was quite an everyday occurrence; but the Church could say with full justification — marriage is a means of grace, but if men refuse to co-operate with grace, it is no use; men have none the less their free will to sin. But to Christian people who believe there is but one perfect good, to possess God, it cannot seem impossible

2 4 3

or unmerciful if they are obliged to consider themselves bound, even by an unhappy marriage.

Even in cases where " hardness of hearts " makes it impossible for husband and wife to live under the same roof — because one of them is cruel, unfaithful, scandalizes the children and brings distress and destitution on the home — among Christians there can only be a question of separation. The partner who considers himself or herself least to blame, or who can say at any rate: I am better able to provide for the wants of the children; they shall not be spectators of their mother's licentious life; they shall not go hungry and be terrified in their own home owing to their father's drunkenness — this one will have enough to do in fulfilling the duties of both parents and making good the neglect of the other party. To a Catholic it will be plain that one party may win merit and offer it for the salvation of the other. If the delinquencies of one party are of such a nature as to render cohabitation impossible the other must nevertheless feel himself, or herself, bound to work for the welfare of both their souls, by prayer and penance and good deeds.

Now it was a cardinal point of the Reformers' doctrine that sexual intercourse is a necessity like food and drink. If celibacy is impossible for priests and monks, it is clear that we cannot demand celibacy of a woman who has to leave her husband in order to save her children's bread or rescue them from brutal treatment. If a man cannot bear to live with a dissolute wife, who drags his and their children's name in the mud, or if his wife has run away — then of course, on Protestant premisses, he cannot be denied the right of taking another wife. Protestants were for that matter perfectly consistent in admitting from the very first the right of divorced persons to remarry. All the more as the discarded partner's " good works " were deprived of their purpose and no longer benefited the soul of either party in the slightest degree.

The inconsistency lay from the first in this, that the Reformers nevertheless clung to tradition and maintained that matrimony was an excellent means of preparing husband and wife for heaven, but only so long as cohabitation was at least endurable.

But ideas of what is endurable and what is not vary with different people and with the people of different ages. In the minds of Christians infidelity is in the first place a *sin;* that is to say, an infidelity to God — or in any case that is how Christians ought to look upon it. And this view has really entered into the Christian tradition of Europe, as a kind of unconscious factor in the estimation of marriage. For a non-Christian woman will not always take a man's infidelity so seriously. If his infidelity means that another woman has taken her place in a man's life — that she has actually been discarded for the sake of another woman — then in the case of most non-Christian women she will never forgive it. But if she is certain that no other woman can ever be what she is to her husband, she really does not worry so very much if her husband now and again embarks on an erotic voyage of discovery elsewhere — unless indeed she is pathologically jealous. If he returns, sheepish and repentant, and tells her the result of his adventure: that now he knows, in an even higher sense than before, that she is the only one for him and the others were nothing — and especially if she can be sure that the other woman has also been made aware of this discovery on the part of the man — then at any rate her pain is softened by other, more pleasant feelings.

In reality a man may offend his wife far more deeply in an infinity of ways — if he avoids aggravating his infidelity by the insult of showing her that she has become indifferent to him. The old Norse sagas, for instance, are concerned with a society in which ordinary men have but *one* wedded wife, and she occupies an honourable position as mother of the family's legitimate children and as sharing the responsibility for the management of its property and household. Both parties can easily obtain a divorce, if dissatisfied with the marriage. But I do not remember a single passage in which we are told that a wife leaves her husband on account of physical infidelity. She may bear hatred to his concubine and bastards. (But Bergthora, in the Njáls Saga, receives Njál's concubine when she comes to the house with the body of her son by Njál; she makes no answer to the abusive words the other mother in her despair flings at the wife, and Bergthora requires of her sons that they avenge their half-brother, for brothers they are.) The sagas show us a different idea of the breaches of faith which justify a wife in leaving her husband — his showing cowardice, committing a dastardly act, failing his own or his wife's kinsmen in a dangerous situation. The laws postulate the right of a wife's kinsmen to take her away from her husband and assume paternal rights over the children, if he fails to provide for his family. For the same reason a man's marriage is dissolved by the mere fact of his being sentenced to " the great outlawry." The wife's kinsmen must come and fetch her, separating her share of the common property. And whether she likes it or not, her marriage with the civilly dead man is at an end. For five nights only may his wife house and help him; if after that they meet in secret, their relations are as it were entirely outside the law; if she has children by him after he has been made an outlaw, they are called " the wolf's cubs " and possess no rights. It is another matter that wives who have the power and the daring put themselves above the law and house their outlawed husbands, just as we hear of mothers housing and aiding their outlawed sons.

Here, in a society based on kinship, the man's infidelity consists in his offending against the welfare and honour of the kin. The woman's fidelity to the kin implies in addition that she be faithful to her husband in a purely physical sense — and that she preserve her purity until the day when her kinsmen solemnly make over its guardianship to a husband. Here the race is the ideal which all individuals are required to serve, and the bearing of all moral ideas is more or less determined by the degree in which the welfare of the race depends on the behaviour of individuals.

If a Christian woman reckons — or ought to reckon

— a man's infidelity to her as so grave a sin, it is because she must see in it a sin against God. And this view has really to a certain extent impressed itself on the traditional European conception — even if many a jealous woman has scarcely been sensible that the most offensive point of the man's infidelity to her was that he offended the religion which she at any rate professed.

Men, of course, have always laid claim to a slightly different — or a very different — kind of fidelity and purity from that of women. And for this Catholic women at least ought to be grateful to them. If it may be said that the only natural morality is that which our aunts called " dual morality " and that it is for us to keep to the stricter sort, we can only say, thanks for the honour. The very nature of sexual relations was responsible for the view almost universally held that the man took, or captured, or bought the woman — his bride became his property in a different way from that in which he became hers. Another thing is that the purity of the family blood depends on its not being tampered with by the women. It is quite extraordinary that of all times in our own day, when science has been able to prove the existence of various types of blood and their hereditability, people should talk gaily about the communistic co-education of children in institutions under the management of strangers. And even people who are not Communists are willing to allow the State power over our children beyond what it has already usurped. And the legislation even of " bourgeois " States moves farther and farther along the lines which can only weaken the union of the family, and looks forward cheerfully to new technical and economic progress which may make it even more difficult to base society upon groups which are bound together by the ties of blood.

3

I ASSUME we Catholics may agree with the more or less radical young people who say that the old form of marriage, which is related in a varying degree with the Christian, Catholic view of matrimony, is unsuitable for our time. What *we* mean is, that the Catholic dogma of marriage is revealed by God; therefore *we* must try to change our time. If on this account we must try to force back the course of development, well, then we must. Not that I know, by the way, why it is to be called " back," but that is how people put it: we must know, then, what we are to aim at. It must be the object of our efforts to defend marriage and family life in those forms which Christ has sanctioned, and as to details we must conform to the rules and precepts and advice given us by His Church.

Those who believe that " evolution " is something mystical, a sort of river under the control of a river god, or under its own control, will presumably do nothing but let themselves drift with the stream — if they are consistent.

But those who believe there is some use in resolving and striving to influence evolution, and who have re-

jected Christianity as a revealed, dogmatic religion —
whether they did so with something like sorrow, holding it to be merely a work of man, a dream, though they
might think it a beautiful dream; or whether they were
actuated by hatred of Christianity — these must inevi-
tably strive to transform marriage, so that it may be
more in accordance with the conditions of the time.

And my intention in writing this article is in the first
place this — to beg Catholics, here in Scandinavia as
elsewhere, to understand that it cannot be otherwise.
We must try to make this clear to ourselves — *we have
no right to assume that any part of European tradition,
cultural values, moral ideas, emotional wealth, which
has its origin in the dogmatically defined Christianity
of the Catholic Church, will continue to live a " natural " life, if the people of Europe reject Christianity and
refuse to accept God's supernatural grace.* One might
just as well believe that a tree whose roots were severed
should continue to bear leaves and blossoms and fruit.

A sentimental clinging to this or that particular section of Christian tradition is of no use. Break off a few
sprigs of a felled tree and put them in vases for indoor
decoration — and see how long they will keep fresh!

It is true that the Church has been able to take over
pre-Christian institutions and moral ideas. And this
" syncretism " within Catholicism is not a survival of
paganism, as bare-bone purists would have it to be, nor
is it flowers that the Church has plucked on her way
among the nations and decked herself with to increase
her attraction — as those try to make out who seek to

explain the Church's mysterious vitality by attributing to her priesthood a shrewdness at least equally mysterious. (We who belong to the Church often think we see desperately little of it!) To us who believe that Christ is " He by whom all things were made " there is of course nothing very remarkable in the fact that the Church was able to take over much of the intellectual inventory of paganism, since every single pagan must bear the mark of the Creator's hand concealed somewhere about him. Adam and Eve *got* what they sinned in order to obtain — the power of knowing good and evil, while at the same time they lost the power of recognizing the absolute good, and acquired the passion for securing all secondary and intermediate good things. Of many of these last the Church could only say, they are good things, and if they become other than good it is only because men hold them to be good *enough*. Normal human beings are always groping after a moral law, and the immoral element in all purely human laws of morality usually lies in their being so fragmentary as to produce the effect of statues composed of odds and ends — essential pieces are wanting, and men were without a model for their reconstruction, until God became man.

Neo-paganism cannot put the clock back, since its starting-point is precisely the rejection of the God-given model, Christ. If it breaks up the whole Christian image of the world, extracts the archaic, pagan elements and presses out of them the Christian juice with which they have become impregnated — it cannot join them together to form a new, organically living body. One can cease to celebrate Yule as the festival of the birth of Christ — one cannot restore to the world the old religious feeling for the sun which gives all and therefore ought to receive something in return as a sacrifice. We can continue to eat the Christmas pig, but that will not bring back the Lord Frey.

Slavery may be reintroduced — we have gone a long way towards it already: industrial capitalism and free competition have resulted in the majority of members of society having lost all security for their economic future. People who own nothing but their capacity for work and have to live by letting it out for daily, weekly, monthly wages or a yearly salary may at any moment be rendered destitute at a word of another person, or as the result of the bad management of a few (usually anonymous) persons. And professional politicians still talk about the nineteenth century having witnessed the liberation of the peoples! It is not surprising if great masses of the people begin to think: if we are to be slaves, then let us anyhow have a slave-owner whose interest it will be that his slaves do not die of want — let there be *one* slave-owner, so that he won't be able to turn us out to die on his neighbour's land, when he has no more use for us — let the State take us!

Slave conditions are accompanied by a renewal of the morality of slavery. This is precisely the point about " comrade-marriage " — it is nothing new, it is as old as the hills: it is the commonest form of sexual intercourse among slaves. As a rule the slave-owner has no reason to meddle with the private erotic affairs of his

slaves, so long as his proprietorship in the offspring is
assured. Free love is for slaves, and marriage is for the
free-born.

In the families of freemen, in a ruling race, it is important to keep the line of descent pure. The daughters
of the free men are presumed to be the bearers of valuable hereditary material; in suing for their hands a man
has to offer substantial compensation; they are handed
over with solemn ceremonies by the representatives of
their own family to the man who is to propagate a ruling race through them. Of a slave-born concubine a man
can demand fidelity so long as he cares to keep her for
himself; of a wife her whole community can demand
fidelity — not because in default of it her husband
might take it into his head to kill her, but because she
shares the responsibility and the honour of the family
with her forefathers and with her husband — or in
spite of her husband, if he is a man without honour —
and with her children.

But does anyone believe that the new slave State
will develop an upper class with a stricter upper-class
morality, based on the idea that certain stocks are fundamentally different from and more valuable than the
masses? It is of course not unlikely that something of the
sort may come about, even in a dechristianized Europe
— that ideas about race hygiene or similar aims may
lead in any case to experiments being made in this
direction.

The Christian Church could not recognize any dual
morality here either — could not acknowledge class

distinctions and racial disparities to be other than trifling variations in a human material which was fundamentally one and the real value of which consisted in something common to all human beings — that God had created them, intending them to be with Him in eternity. The Church could not affirm that slavery in itself was degrading to the *slaves:* the acts of the martyrs in the first centuries of Christianity gave superabundant evidence that the lot of a slave *need* not debase a person's soul or take away its freedom. The souls of the slave-owners were in a worse case. But the Church insisted that Christian slave-owners should at least refrain from hindering their slaves' participation in the Church's means of grace, among them the sacrament of marriage. In making this demand and in recognizing the cohabitation of slaves as marriage according to ecclesiastical law, even if civil society refused to give it any juridical legitimacy, the Church perhaps did more to abolish the slavery of the ancient world than by any other means at her disposal. Little by little the Church's view gained prevalence all over Europe — the right of living in matrimony and founding a family is a human privilege which may be voluntarily renounced by individual men and women, but it is criminal for other people, or social conditions, to withhold it.

Where Christianity penetrated in Europe, it had in any case this to build upon: in that part of the population which was free the family was theoretically held in honour and acknowledged to be the foundation on which society must be based. If they could do nothing else, those men who felt a responsibility for the destiny of their nation lamented the decay of family life — as in Rome under the Empire, when legislators sought for means of regenerating the ideal family life on which the greatness of the Roman people was assumed to have been founded. The doctrine of the Church, which raised marriage from a contract to a sacrament, involved new consequences which must have seemed fairly revolutionary: it taught that marriage was entered into by mutual consent, thus acknowledging, in theory at any rate, that a woman could not be given away against her will; it taught that the husband owed his wife fidelity in precisely the same sense as she was bound to be faithful to him; and the slaves' right to a family life, which had been admitted in practice, when it did not conflict too sharply with the master's interests, was asserted as absolute. But the nations were to some extent prepared to accept the Church's doctrine of the sanctity of marriage and the primary place of the fourth commandment among God's rules for human relations, inasmuch as the contractual relation between a man and a woman, marriage, was already important and involved responsibility in many directions, and was thus held in honour. A man's irregular connections were essentially his own affair and therefore were normally regarded as trifles. And the fourth commandment merely gave divine sanction and explanation to much that had already formed the base of the ruling families' morality in pre-Christian times. In those sections of the people which had any property at all, the family was really the unit which owned the property and kept together like a co-operative society.

Nowadays, as everyone knows, economic conditions are such that the natural family has little material encouragement to keep together on rational considerations, unless impelled to do so by religious conviction. On the contrary, anyone who is at all acquainted with conditions in ordinary Catholic homes — and not only those that are downright poor, but also Catholic middle-class homes — knows that in many cases nothing less than heroism is required if husband and wife really desire to live together as a good Christian couple. It calls for a self-discipline, a habit of self-conquest, which normally is not acquired without much prayer and a diligent use of the Sacraments, if two modern people are to continue fond of each other and to show patience and evenness of temper every time one of them intentionally or otherwise says something unkind or " gets on the other's nerves." On every hand echoes reach them from a world which tries to base marriage upon " mutual respect and affection." (It must be remembered that in a democratic community the general public always lives on ideas which twenty or thirty years ago were the peculiar property of a few " advanced minds " — and which the most " advanced " people of the moment have discarded as unserviceable working hypotheses.) Alas, it is a good thing that the ordinary average male so seldom knows to what extent his ordinary average wife has seen through him in the course of, let us say, ten years of married life. Presumably it is also a good thing that very few average wives know what their husbands have thought of them in ten years of marriage. There is no getting away from the fact that very few people would be able to endure each other if they were not bound together to serve some ideal which is so great as to make them both seem equally insignificant when measured against it. And it is impossible to advocate lifelong monogamy unless one believes that every single human soul is worth God's dying to save it.

Nothing but this belief can justify the Catholic idea of marriage. No other belief can give the people of our day courage to live according to nature and accept the children that God gives them, except this — the belief that every child has a soul which is worth more than the whole visible, created world. Read the ladies' papers and you will see to what extent it is taken for granted, precisely by the broad middle class — which is progressive and self-respecting and has boundless confidence in its own enlightenment and its own morality — that children are a pleasure which one ought to allow oneself, since people have paternal and maternal instincts which ought not to remain unsatisfied. But one must limit the number of children according to one's means: no more than one can give a good start in life to! So they shake their heads at the Catholic mother — good gracious, another? well, some people have no sense of responsibility! And the Catholic mother knows that every child she has is worth more than all the stars in the heavens, though at times she is near fainting under the shower of stars. It keeps her tied within the walls of her home

— and it may seem tempting when she sees other mothers who have their well-paid work outside the home and can afford competent help, so that their houses and children look better cared for than her own. While the father is prematurely worn and middle-aged in his struggle to provide the greedy little stars with their bread and margarine.

There is however one side of the matter to which no very great attention appears to have been devoted in the discussion on " birth control." It is natural enough that young people, the first time they feel disappointed with the world and their fellow-creatures, should turn round to their parents and yelp: " I didn't ask for life " — " why did you bring me into the world? " Formerly parents could decline to answer — could leave their children to find out for themselves. But now? When it is preached far and wide that only those who are " fitted for it " should bring children into the world; nay more, only those who in their own opinion " are qualified to give their children a good bringing-up." God have mercy on them when they have to face the criticism of their offspring! People are to limit the number of their children to so many as they think they can afford to give a good start in life. God have pity on them when their children have to go through a time of depression! Where will these parents find a hole to hide in if their children confront them with awkward interpellations?

The fact is, of course, that in all this talk about birth control, " optional motherhood," and society's need of more children or fewer children or children with defi-

2 5 8

nite hereditary aptitudes, there is one party who for sufficient reasons is unable to have his say. For it is notorious that no means exists of safeguarding optional
childhood, or of inquiring of children yet unconceived
or unborn whether they are willing to enter society and
take upon themselves the tasks that await them.

What, for instance, will the victims of some people's
appetite for optional motherhood and fatherhood say,
when they have to take up the burdens that their parents have prepared for them? All the charitable work
which the Church began for Christ's sake, and which
millions of people, religious and lay, have given their
lives and welfare to keep going, has been taken over to
a great extent by secularized society, which thought it
could do it better: thus the objects of this charitable
work — sick persons, destitute orphans, defectives, old
people past work, and so on — were no longer called
upon to be grateful for aid which they received as a
matter of simple justice. (The Church too regarded it
as no more than just — but she considered that men
are very far from finding it so natural to practise justice
as to render gratitude superfluous when justice has been
done.) Moreover, in talking about justice we Europeans always more or less consciously have in our minds
Christian justice. Christian justice knows in what way
it is related to charity. Just as we have in our minds
Christian truth when we are enthusiastic about truth-
fulness. In reality pagan justice is harsh enough, and
unchristianized truth is both cruel and shameless.

The result of the artificial limitation of children is

already beginning to show itself, amongst other ways in the fact that the percentage of the population which is young, of full working age, and which by the surplus of its labour has to assist that part of the nation which is wholly or partly incapacitated, is growing smaller than it has ever been in historical times. So we shall see how willing this generation — which knows that its parents have practised limitation of the number of their children, but unlimited contracting of debts and unlimited nationalization of the burdens which formerly rested on the family and which the Church took up voluntarily — is to sustain the heritage of its parents.

4

Our Catholic children too will have to share the responsibility for the solution of all the problems which have been piled up for the next generation, in communities where Christian principles have long been left out of consideration by administrators and legislators. No one will deny that avarice, a passion for material enjoyment, vanity and a desire of personal success were widely prevalent even at the time when the power of the Church was at its highest. Priests and prelates took part in the struggle for material benefits, one monastic community after another grew too rich and degenerated into materialism. But it is only our right to remember that in a Catholic community materialism has never been recognized as an *ideal* — and people who pursued such ideals were in any case intellectually honest enough not to compose delightful theories which might excuse their greed; they had the redeeming impudence necessary for admitting: I am like this because I wish to be like this, and that's an end of it. The ideal continued to be the person who can dispense with this world as far as possible — and let us not forget that for every religious Order which broke down under the weight of its wealth, a new one sprang up and grasped the ancient banner — and as a rule a new and stricter Order received such support that the very numbers of those who flocked to it made it difficult to uphold the ancient ideal. Catholicism fought against Manicheism and the heresy of the Albigenses, as heresy, since these systems taught that matter is evil in itself, the work not of God, but of the devil — but it has fought, and must go on fighting to the end of time, to keep materialism in its place, under the dominion of the spirit. St. Francis speaks of his sister the earth, as though she were a sweet baby sister whom he caresses on his way to his work.

But it is a new thing — and in the main a product of Calvinism — that in our day it is held to be meritorious to acquire a steadily growing fortune, a worthy object of human effort to make a name for oneself which will live for centuries (might not St. Francis have thought this a curious ambition for an immortal soul!) [1] and success is held to be a thing which ought to inspire respect. It is good Catholicism to put one's country's wel-

---

[1] As Christopher Hollis remarks with reference to Stanton's words about the dead Lincoln: " Now he belongs to the ages."

fare higher than one's own life, but it is not Catholic to put one's country's welfare above the cause of Christianity — poisonous nationalism is un-Catholic, as patriotism is Catholic.

I suppose no one will go so far as to pretend that legislation in Scandinavia, in all that concerns marriage and family life, has had the slightest consideration for the principles of Christianity. So long as I was not a Christian I too regarded marriage as a contract which in certain circumstances could be dissolved. But if one has once decided to disregard Christian principles I am not sure that the harem system, for instance, does not offer material advantages over the system on which plurality of wives and of husbands is now practised in Northern Europe; amongst other things it ensures better cohesion among blood relations and makes it less easy for a man who has reached the forties to throw out his aging wife and marry a young girl. If elderly gentlemen insist on marrying young girls — and it is a very common passion which Christianity has had great trouble in keeping in check — there is a good deal to be said in favour of their taking the girls as secondary wives. Of course this is not ideal — as a Mohammedan friend of mine admitted; one day in Paris he had been praising his people's stricter morals and greater care for women's real welfare. But it would not be easy to find anything more ideal, if one is to abandon the ideal of Christianity. Perhaps one might find serviceable ideas in India — without going to the extremes of child-marriage, which Miss Mayo has exposed. But for my own part I would prefer an arrangement which limits the freedom of women as that of plants in a field is limited, to one which liberates them as billets are liberated from a log by axe and by saw — to be thrown upon the pile, from whence they will find their way into a furnace in which at any rate they cannot be said to be " bound."

We Catholics in Scandinavia are few in number, and our congregations are poor, and most of us have neither time nor facilities for keeping pace with what is being done by our coreligionists on the continent of Europe. We have to do the best we can. Our little handful of students must try to penetrate to the core of our own civilization, to form an idea of the significance of the Catholic Church's contribution to civilization — to understand what in the intellectual life and social structure of Europe during the last two thousand years is not a fruit of natural human development, but a result of men having accepted God's revelation in Jesus Christ and worked under the grace of His Holy Spirit.

It is of course even more important that we all accept this revelation *now,* and that we humbly acknowledge we can do nothing that is good and lasting unless we pray for His Spirit and try to allow it scope to work within us — without offering resistance when it attacks that in us which is our own and which we love egoistically, and without wishing to reserve any room or closet within us and put a notice on the door: No admittance for Christ. But in this it is the business of our priests to help each one of us. And this work will be the same for all — educated and uneducated, talented and untalented, young and old, parents and children.

But I should like to ask all my coreligionists to remember two things — our Catholic families are not well off, and it is the duty of all of us to do everything we can to support and help our brothers and sisters in their struggle to maintain a home.

The second thing is — the problem of our children's schooling is a burning one. The burning problem everywhere in Europe is: what can we do in the whole of Christendom to provide our children with Catholic education in Catholic schools? We cannot make use of schools in which religion is treated as one subject among many — and in which the other subjects are treated as though there were any human activity or any factors in human life which were purely secular. We must teach our children that God is the only goal of our life, that life has no other purpose than learning to know Him, preparing, while we live on earth, to be admitted to see Him — to see that Vision which is bliss.

Otherwise I must admit I do not think life can be very interesting in the long run. We may, if we please, look on it as a workshop — but the work is so irritating in its poorness and its stupid organization, its directors introduce so much foolery that with very few exceptions they really deserve hanging. That is, if we do not think we all make a mess of the tasks allotted to us and have need of God's mercy. Or of course one may try to look on life as a festivity — as a rule one gets bored with it before very long. One need not show it, naturally, because after all it is a family festivity, so it is better man-

ners to pretend it is a success — though one is always
tempted to steal away when it is getting late; if one does
so nicely the others will not pay much attention, those
who are really enjoying themselves (if they do really enjoy themselves) won't notice if one guest disappears. —
Unless one believes, as we believe, that this world is the
starting-point for a journey into Eternity. —

Finally — let us remember that Christ has promised
His Church that the gates of Hell shall not prevail
against it. We believe that the Church of Christ will
subsist on earth as long as human life stirs on this globe.
But it is nowhere promised us that our continent and
the nations with which we are related shall continue to
belong to the Church of Christ through all the ages.
The Church militant on earth may be reduced to a
handful of adherents, not many more than would fill
an arena or a local jail. The Christians of Europe may
be reduced to a little band with no power to influence
social development for a long period — reduced to play
a part something like that of the English Catholics in
the eighteenth century. Until Catholic missionaries,
from China or South America or Africa, return to
preach the faith of our fathers to the lost barbarian
tribes who are living amongst the ruins of ancient
Europe.

Well, now I have been as pessimistic as I could be —
or am, when I picture to myself the nations following
different lines to which they have tied themselves down.
The world may witness that the whole course of development may take another direction — or be given an-

other direction. But we Catholics will do well to remember that Our Lord saved the world by not sparing His Only-begotten Son. And even if what He has left us to do is really trifles — like the pretence that parents may let their little children do when they are supposed to be " helping father and mother " — it may seem hard enough to us poor sinful men and women.

In this connection I have entirely left out of account the contribution of the Protestant sects. Not that I have any doubt that many individual Protestant Christians are fighting, each for himself, for the ancient standards of Christendom. But as organized ecclesiastical communities almost all Protestant sects, at any rate in the question of marriage and family life, have capitulated to the pagan views. In this matter, as in so many others, they have " moved with the times "; that is, they have caught hold of the tail of the garment of " evolution " and held on to it, allowing themselves to be pulled along, while imagining that they held the reins.